Sell Your Screenplay offers advice from an experienced and gutsy screenwriter. With hundreds of valuable contacts and resources, this empowering, must-read guide is for both beginning and professional screenwriters. Without an agent the author had to promote herself. She graciously teaches you how to do the same! Follow her courageous journey through the sale of her first spec script and learn to find the help you need to succeed in this ultra-competitive business.

Praise for *Sell Your Screenplay* . . .

"Ms. Wolf has written an invaluable book, filled with astute, detailed advice, and priceless contact information. Aspiring screenwriters should follow this one writer's journey to her first screenplay sale if they are serious about finding success of their own."
> —Michael B. Druxman, Screenwriter-Director

"I'm a full time novelist/screenwriter who teaches screenwriting in San Francisco, where Andrea Wolf was a former student. Her book is a valuable, practical addition to the myriad of screenwriting books. It offers insights from a talented writer, supplies option agreements and release forms, and provides extensive lists of independent production companies and screenwriting competitions that are available to the newcomer. I highly recommend it for aspiring screenwriters."
> —James Dalessandro, Screenwriter/Author

More praise for *Sell Your Screenplay* . . .

"When dealing with Hollywood and all its aspects, you can't know it all. Andrea Wolf has done all the footwork for you in her book. Because of her thoroughness and just because *she* did it, I had the courage to pursue my dream. Through her book, she encouraged me to *do it*! If she could do it, I could, too. And I did. This little ol' housewife/screenwriter from North Idaho got optioned! Take this book and make it your screenwriting bible. It is truly the last and *most complete* word on how someone from 'outside' of Hollywood can get a foot 'inside.' This is your best guide to a star-studded career."

—Cheryl Rovang, Screenwriter

"One of the most comprehensive listings of independent film producers and production companies I've seen. If you're ready to start selling your screenplay, I highly recommend you check out the listings in this book!"

—Christopher Wehner, Screenwriter's Utopia.com

Gotta Minute? ™

Sell Your Screenplay

Your guide to the independent film and television producer

Andrea Leigh Wolf

Robert D. Reed Publishers • San Francisco, California

Robert D. Reed Publishers
750 La Playa Street, Suite 647
San Francisco, CA 94121
Phone: 650-994-6570 • Fax: 650-994--6579
E-mail: 4bobreed@msn.com
Web site: www.rdrpublishers.com

Editor, Typesetter, and Co-publisher:
   Pamela D. Jacobs, M.A.
Assistant Editor:
   Ruth Schenkel
Cover Designer:
   Julia A. Gaskill

ISBN 1-885003-47-1

Library of Congress Catalogue Number: 00-100654

Manufactured, Typeset, and Printed in the United States

For my husband, Darrell, who always believed in my dream and my need to fulfill it.

For our granddaughters, Jessica Nicole and Crystal Marina, who are the stars in my sky.

And for Ray Robinson, the independent producer who took his valuable time to turn me into the screenwriter I wanted to be. Thank you.

Disclaimer

This book is sold with the understanding that the subject matter covered herein is of a general nature and does not constitute professional advice for any specific individual or situation. Readers planning to take action in any of the areas that this book describes should seek professional advice from their own attorneys, agents, or other advisers—as would be prudent and advisable under their given circumstances.

Contents

Preface – vi

Introduction – viii

The Spec Script – 1

My Dream Is Born – 5

My Path Begins – 9

The Pitch – 12

Submitting My First Script – 15

Reader's Report – 22

On My Own – 32

The Business of Screenwriting – 39

Meeting Hollywood Insiders Outside of Hollywood – 41

When You Option Your Script – 46

The Independent Producer (Your Gateway to Success) – 66

Meet Independent Film and TV Producers – 68

List of Independent Film and TV Producers – 75

Film Commissions – 117

Standard Release Forms – 123

Collaboration Agreements – 127

Screenplay Competitions – 134

Trade Publications – 146

Film Industry Organizations – 148

Web Connections for Screenwriters -- 150

Script Doctors – 160

After You Sell Your Script – 163

Glossary – 165

About The Author – 168

Preface

On November 7, 1995, I signed on the dotted line, transforming myself from a "wannabe" into a "professional" screenwriter. Just three days earlier I had sent my spec script, *Nowhere To Hide* (a true crime drama based on a crime that my family and I survived), in response to an ad in *Variety*.

A producer loved *Nowhere To Hide* but felt the script was more bloody and violent than he was looking for. But he loved my writing and asked what else I had.

In Hollywood, no matter how much they love your script, they always ask, "What else do you have?" So I sent him *Pegasus* (*Home Alone* meets *ET*), a family script I had recently completed. He looked over it, but just couldn't let go of *Nowhere To Hide*. A few days later he called to ask, "Would you mind if I take *Nowhere To Hide* back to Los Angeles with me?"

It took me about a second to respond, "Sure, no problem."

I had no idea that when he said, ". . . back to Los Angeles . . ." he meant "Paramount Ranch" and that he actually worked for CBS. Or that when he said he worked for "The Eye," he meant he worked on what was a top CBS series at the time. (In Hollywood you rarely know to whom you are talking—people don't wear signs on their chests.) I was unaware that, like a growing number of Hollywood insiders, he lived outside of L.A. and commuted back and forth. He was looking for his first feature project to produce under his own independent production company.

Less than a week later he called me from Los Angeles and said "I'm getting a lot of 'buzz' on *Nowhere To Hide*. I'd like to option it."

Less than twenty-four hours later, he called again to "exercise his option." He said, "I'd like to buy *Nowhere To Hide*."

At first I wasn't sure what he meant, having heard so many promises before. But up to that moment no one had uttered those sweet words, "I'd like to exercise my option."

I had done it! I had achieved what screenplay marketing books claimed could not be done. I had sold my first spec script without an agent. To top it off, it was the first script I had ever written. I had found a "back door"—the Independent Producer.

I really enjoyed making my own contacts and meeting all of the successful people in the film business. I wasn't interested in using them—instead, I wanted to study and learn from them. I was marketing my own work and loved it. I had kept a journal of everything I had done from day one—conversations with people, contracts received, what worked and what didn't. I had been there. Who else could write about what I had been through? Who else could know what it had been like to market my script? I had been in the trenches and I wanted to share my experiences and information with other beginning screenwriters.

I write all the time and I love it! My advice to others is this: if you don't have a passion for writing, if you don't live and breathe writing for film, and if that passion doesn't fill your soul, find something else to do with your time—something easier. If you're writing for the potential money and success and not purely for the love of it, it will show in your writing. Studio readers will sense a lack of passion in your script, discard it, and move on to the next one.

Introduction

Sell Your Screenplay is for screenwriters who are working *without* an agent, who live outside of the Hollywood area, and who may live in small, out-of-the-way towns all over the world. Any screenwriter can take advantage of this book by learning from my mistakes and my successes. Most importantly, they can learn how to sell their own work!

Thousands of fledgling screenwriters have submitted great story ideas to Hollywood, but most of their scripts have landed in wastepaper baskets. Why? Although their scripts may have the potential to become the next *Titanic* or *Saving Private Ryan*, "wannabe" screenwriters lack the basic skills or knowledge that it takes to market scripts. The biggest challenge for screenwriters is inspiring people to commit millions of dollars toward producing their scripts.

As a beginning screenwriter you may not know how to get the attention of Hollywood producers. You don't necessarily have to live in Hollywood to sell your first script, but you must know the "business of Hollywood." You must have some idea of what producers are looking for before you submit your script. You may want to study the current *Spec Script Sales Directory* by Howard Meilbach, which keeps newcomers abreast of what's going on in the spec script market. (A spec script is one you write on your own without a commitment from anyone to read it, buy it, or produce it.) Do your homework. It will show. It takes more than writing talent. It takes marketing ability and knowledge of what the "Business of Hollywood" is all about.

I decided to write *Sell Your Screenplay* after people kept asking me, "How did you do it?" I had my journal and I thought, why not? (Much of this book comes from my journal.) I wanted to share with other writers what it took for me to sell my first spec script, how I sold it without an agent or a Hollywood connection, and how that first sale led to even more credits.

Let's assume you have already completed your first spec script and have started writing your second one. And let's assume that your script is polished and in pristine presentation form—it's the best it can be. If so, you have completed one-quarter of the scriptwriting process. Now the fun begins . . . with Marketing. Unfortunately, it's the marketing process that makes or breaks most screenwriters. It's the strong and determined screenwriter who will survive.

Be prepared. There will be many rejections. I wish I could say that you will only experience rejections in the beginning, but you won't. Even after you've sold your first script, the rejections will continue. It's part of the marketing process— each and every script goes through it. There will be many "no" responses to your queries. That's typical. Just remember it's not personal. Your success, or lack of it, will depend on you and how you handle the rejections. If you don't make it, you have only yourself to blame.

Writers often misinterpret the purpose of networking. They think they can find insiders who will take their scripts and market and sell them without the slightest effort on their part. In reality, contacts may open a door or two, but it's up to the writers to arrange meetings and pitch their own ideas. Don't expect anyone to pick up your tab for hotels, airfare, meals, transportation, and other expenses while you are marketing your script. So break out the plastic (credit cards). Once you make it (and you must believe you will), many expenses should be taken care of. You must be completely committed to your career and learn to avoid pitfalls.

My hope is that this book will help you through the rough times—the times when you feel most alone in this process. I've included suggestions, useful information and resources, samples of contracts I received, and lessons learned from difficulties that tripped me up when I was starting out. I did not interview industry insiders and put their views in this book. Instead, this book is based on my own experiences and is intended to help you be more prepared than I was.

"Still," you say, "I don't live in Hollywood." That doesn't necessarily have to hinder your success. I don't live there either. That's why I wrote this book—to help bridge the miles between your home office and the independent film producer.

Consider that you are an entrepreneur in business for yourself. When your script is completed you must take on another role, that of an agent. You are selling what you know best—yourself and your talent. You must also become your own business manager, cheerleader, and therapist (you may need to be in this final role most of all).

You must love the movies to write for the movies. Whenever I am sitting in a movie theater I feel moved as the screenwriting credits appear on the screen. Most movies draw me in instantly and I begin living the story along with the characters—allowing myself to escape everyday life and become someone else or go someplace else. I don't get distracted while watching films by searching for production errors or analyzing the story lines.

When I write screenplays I recall the sense of absorption in the story I have as a part of the audience. I visualize each scene as I write it. If I don't see it in my mind and don't care about the characters, I throw away what I have written and start over. After all, if I don't care about the characters or the story, how will the producer, director, actors, or audience care about them?

Remember, there are *many* ways for you to market your script. Do whatever works. When one way fails, try another. Use the information in this book to save time and avoid making mistakes while marketing your screenplay to the independent market. Good luck!

Now, get ready to learn how to sell your screenplay!

Guidelines for your road to success:

1. Be Aggressive.
2. Be Relentless.
3. Be Tenacious.
4. Be Professional.

The Spec Script

A "spec" script is written without a commitment from anyone but yourself. It is written "on spec" (speculation). No one has agreed to read it, buy it, or produce it. You are writing on your own with high hopes of someday selling your work. It should be your best writing sample because it is your calling card script—an introduction to your work. The writing of a spec is an art form. Beginning screenwriters who keep this in mind will avoid many problems down the road.

Many scripts I have critiqued have been overwritten. The writers used excessive narrative/action and meaningless dialogue. Dialogue that does not move the story forward should not be in the script. (You hear this a lot.) Even the greatest dialogue may be inappropriate or have nothing to do with the plot. If so, get rid of it.

Your spec script should be mostly dialogue. This is where your character development really needs to shine. Do not have the characters standing around with nothing to do or say. Most beginning screenwriters clutter their scripts with unnecessary chatter, wasting valuable screen time. Remember, you only have 120 pages. Each page of your script is a minute on the screen. Make every minute count.

The most important person who will read your script is the reader (the first professional person reading your script). If you fail to pull the reader into your story from page one, and most certainly by page ten, it will not get any further up the studio ladder.

A spec script must be "visual." The words in your screenplay must create images in the reader's mind. Choose your words carefully. Turn your words into pictures.

As the spec scriptwriter, you are the most important element in what will become a collaborative effort. The other creative people, such as the cinematographers, directors, etc., will work to combine their talents to produce the completed film. Your job as the writer is to create the skeleton of the story. If you've done your job well, the other talented people will add the flesh of the story and bring it to life.

With that said, the story itself lies within your creative realm—the drama, the characterization, all of it. You must create a compelling story with believable characters. This way the actors and other talents can build on your written words and bring your story and characters to life.

Beginning scriptwriters tend to have problems with formatting and packaging. Such scripts may scream "newcomer!" Scripts sold at outlets (such as Script City, etc.) are great teaching tools, but for the most part they are not spec scripts. They are "shooting scripts" (scripts used while filming). Don't use them as "format" guides when writing your spec script. Those scripts are more helpful for learning story structure, dialogue, and the pacing of your spec script.

When writing your spec script, do not use camera angles, POV (point of view), cut to's, fade in's, and fade out's repeatedly throughout your script. Use one FADE IN in the beginning and one FADE OUT at the end. A good reason not to use camera angles and other directives is that by using them incorrectly you could distract or even turn off your reader.

When choosing card stock for the cover of your script, do not select one with excessive artwork or one that is too brightly colored. You want your script to stand out because of the writing, not because it has a gaudy cover. Pictures or a loud cover will mark you as a "novice." If you were Aaron Sorken (*A Few Good Men*) you could write a script on a cocktail napkin. But you're not. You're just beginning your career so you want your work to look professional.

In the beginning, stick to the basic spec script format. Develop your script and create an interesting read, a real page-turner. Give the reader a great roller-coaster ride—a reason to continue reading, rather than toss your script aside and move on to someone else's script. Whether or not the reader continues reading your script depends on you.

The format of spec scripts will change from time to time, so keep current. As the expression goes, *"You only get one chance to make a good first impression."* Don't spoil your chance by sending in a script that is not up to current industry standards.

Think of the writing of your script as a game in which the object is to turn on your reader. Tell the best story you can. Begin your script dramatically and build from there. Carefully choose your words. In screenwriting, less is more.

Your spec script must be a fast, smooth read. Use no more than four lines of narration/action per paragraph. If you must use more, be sure to separate the four-line paragraphs by a space. Sentences should be brief. Sometimes only one word is needed to make your point. If you use the right word, that will be all you need. Make your writing clear and lively.

I can't say enough about the reader. He or she is the single most important person who will read your script. Don't forget that. It is through this individual that your script will get its chance.

As a beginning writer, don't think for a moment that the experienced, professional writers didn't make the same mistakes that you may be making now. Most did.

That being said, let's get down to business. Maybe I can help speed up the path to your first sale.

The First Ten Pages

The first ten pages of your script are one-third of your first act. These are the most important pages of your spec script. That's because most readers won't read further if they are not into your story by page ten. Recently I spoke with some professional readers who said they will not read beyond page three if they aren't into the story. By page three they can already tell whether or not the writer can write.

Beginning scriptwriters often try to cram all of their story into the first ten pages. Pacing is everything. Tease your reader. Give the reader just enough to pull him or her in. Make each word count.

Study your favorite film. Do you know how much of what you're seeing on the screen actually appeared on the page of the script? Remember what I said earlier about screenwriting being a collaborative effort? Many creative people look at your script and envision your original scenes different ways, bringing their own visions to the scenes. They flesh out your scenes. Then there's the director's input, which may be entirely different.

Take a hard look at your script. If you can see one or more of the problems that I have pointed out, you are ready for a rewrite.

As I like to say, *"Dreams don't just happen. We make them happen."*

My Dream Is Born

Pessimists say that dreams don't come true. Fortunately, I'm an optimist and know that dreams can become a reality if you're willing and determined enough to pursue them. I'm living proof. I'm also happy to share with you how I did it. To begin with, I've always loved the magic of film. Maybe that's why I've been able to stay focused on my dream. My parents took me to my first film at age five and I have been hooked ever since.

We were living in Tampa, Florida. The theater was amazing. It was half indoors and half outdoors. We sat under the stars. It was magical.

After the film began I never moved an inch. It was *The Dolly Sisters*, a musical starring John Payne, Betty Grable, June Haver, Reginald Gardiner, Frank Latimore, and S.Z. Sakall. I'll never forget the title song, "I Can't Begin To Tell You." In the flashy, vaudeville musical comedy, Grable and Haver played song-and-dance sisters. It was the best love story I've ever seen on the silver screen. In my opinion, John Payne was (and still is) the king of "B" movies.

Years later, when I began to seriously pursue a professional writing career, I wanted to contact the actor who had had such an impact on my life. Tenaciously, I queried John Payne about writing his biography. I couldn't believe that no one had done so before. He was one of the greatest actors Hollywood had ever seen. In my opinion he was better than Clark Gable. In my letter I mentioned how much I had admired his work and how I believed that he was never truly appreciated in Hollywood.

Imagine my surprise when John Payne called me one Sunday morning! He was the most gracious man with whom I had ever had the pleasure of speaking. He sounded just as he had the first time I had seen him on film. We talked for a long time. He inquired about my writing and even my family.

Sadly, as flattered as he was, he wasn't ready to write his biography. He said he'd be ready in ten or fifteen years, so if I were still interested then . . . . Two short years later, John Payne was killed in an unfortunate accident. I will never forget his kindness and this meaningful connection.

I mention this experience to you because John Payne's phone call inspired me very much. When he died suddenly, it occurred to me how often we delay things until it's too late. I knew then that I wanted to become a part of the film industry that was so important to me.

How many times have you thought or said, "I'm going to write a book someday?" Well, there's no time like the present. Life passes by too quickly.

Every year while watching the Academy Awards, I dream of the day that I will accept my own Oscar for "Best Original Screenplay." It has never occurred to me that I will not get an Oscar. In fact, when I began writing, my husband bought me a replica of an Oscar while he was on a business trip. It caused quite a stir at the security point at O'Hare Airport. A security guard held it up and pretended to accept the award. Travelers waiting in line cheered and laughed during his "acceptance speech."

When our children became young adults, my husband, Darrell, told me, "It's your turn to pursue your dream. Go for it!"

Around that time a famous, prolific mystery author, Marciel Baker (aka Marcia Miller), walked into the beauty salon where I was working and changed my life forever. She was a walk-in (didn't have an appointment) and I was the only one available to help her. Was that a "sign"? I think so.

Marciel had more than forty published novels to her credit. We talked as I shampooed her hair, and one thing led to another. I told her about the 850-page unpublished, historical romance novel that I had in my hope chest. I had written this novel when I was sixteen years old. Marciel was so impressed that she and her husband, also a famous writer, A.A. Baker, said that when they returned from New York in two weeks, they would like to read my manuscript.

I was so excited that I canceled the rest of my appointments that day. I went home and dug the manuscript out from my hope chest and began to read it. It was rough, written in longhand, and written with all the romantic sentimentality that a teenager with raging hormones would feel. It was so visual that I could picture each and every scene. I was thinking like a screenwriter. That's what I really wanted, to see it on the big screen. But, I didn't know where to start. I didn't know anyone in Hollywood. Truth be known, I didn't even own a typewriter.

My husband had never realized how much I wanted to write until that day. I was never one to whine, "Poor little me. I'm not getting to do what I want."

I don't know whether it was Marciel's interest in my writing or the fact that she was famous and was taking an interest in me, but her interest led me to believe that it was time to begin my journey.

Because we lived so far from Hollywood there were no screenwriting groups with which I could get involved. I didn't know any writers other than the Bakers. Knowing that I didn't want to write novels but still wanted to be around other writers, the Bakers took me to a meeting of the Mystery Writers of America in San Francisco. There I met several famous authors who took great interest in me and offered to help because the Bakers introduced me as their protegé.

At home I joined a local romance writer's group. Members told me there was no way I could break into Hollywood. They said that my best chance would be to write romance novels, and that maybe someday, someone would recognize my name in Hollywood and I would get my chance.

I had never enjoyed romance novels much but I did as they advised. For seven years, I tried to write something (that I hated) and got nowhere. Major editors would write to me and some would even call. They said I had a lot of talent, but not for romance novels. I will always be grateful to those editors for directing me to quit the romance novel business and write what I really wanted to write—what I had a great passion to write—screenplays.

While writing romance novels, I had earned published credits and a few dollars (very few) along the way. I wrote some nonfiction articles for the local newspaper. I was given my own column in *Amazing Experiences* magazine as a movie critic. I would review science fiction films under "Movie Moments with Andrea." Still, I wasn't writing screenplays.

I was haunted by the underlying question, "How will I become a professional screenwriter when I'm not living in Hollywood?" The answer? By using every option available to me. By making my own way. By setting my own rules. By finding a "back door." The same would have held true whether I lived in Northern California or anywhere else in the world.

This book is a journal of my path. It will show you what did and did not work for me. It will show you how to make Hollywood come to you, no matter where you live.

My Path Begins

My dream had always been to sit in a movie theater and suddenly see across the wide screen: *"An Andrea Leigh Wolf Film."* But I had never had any concept of how to make that happen. All the cards seemed stacked against me. I didn't live in Hollywood. I didn't have any relatives or friends in the film business. I wasn't even a film student. I had never heard of any screenwriting classes or seminars in my area and didn't even know a screenwriter. And I thought I was too old.

What I did have was an unyielding determination to make it as a professional screenwriter and a built-in belief that I could beat the odds—not by waiting around for someone to help me, but by doing it myself and creating my own breaks.

Then it happened! One day in early 1988 a friend called. A Hollywood producer with major industry credits was coming to Sacramento to hold a one-day workshop at American River College. It was J. Kenneth Rotcop. This was a perfect example of Hollywood coming to me. I didn't know it then but he was about to open a door to Hollywood for me. The following blurb appeared in the local paper: "Television writer, Ken Rotcop, will conduct a one-day seminar/workshop Friday on how to write a screenplay." (Mr. Rotcop was the single most influential person I'd met in those early years of my career. He gave me the courage to go after my dream.)

J. Kenneth Rotcop had written and produced *For Us The Living: The Story of Medgar Evers*. He'd won the Writers Guild Award, the Image Award, and the Neil Simon Award. He had been honored by Filmex, Women In Film, the National Democratic Party, the NAACP, and the State of Mississippi. He had produced the comedy feature film *Bikini Shop*. He wrote *Killshop* for Samuel Goldwyn Studios and "The Arcade" for Columbia Pictures TV. He had sold a TV series to ABC, *Ruby and Samuel*, through New World Productions. During his career he had been Creative Head of three studios: Embassy Pictures, under Joseph E. Levine; Trans-World Productions; and Hanna-Barbera Productions. He had created and produced the pilot for the highly acclaimed television series *Couples* with D. Walter Brockelman. *The Magic Shop* was another writer/producer credit for him. "Images and Attitudes," the first show dealing with Black-American History, won Mr. Rotcop the Unity Award for Excellence in writing. He had written for every form of television—including talk shows, variety shows, political shows, Saturday morning animation, sitcoms, and dramas.

After learning so much about the man who would bring Hollywood to Sacramento I was determined to go to the workshop. My boss, however, felt otherwise. I had a day job and, although I tried everything short of quitting, I was unable to get that day off. It was heartbreaking. I could not believe I would have to miss such an extremely important screenwriting workshop facilitated by such an accomplished Hollywood insider. I was devastated.

But that was not the last I would hear from Mr. Rotcop. I had missed the workshop but, to my surprise, a month later I received an unbelievable invitation in the mail. The envelope had a Los Angeles return address and was addressed to me! I ripped open the envelope with shaky hands. It was from Mr. Rotcop himself, and it read: "I was sorry to hear that you were unable to attend my workshop."

Teary-eyed, I continued to read.

He wrote: "I would be delighted to have you participate in any of my upcoming workshops or seminars as my guest. If you'll just let me know ahead of time when you'd like to come down, I'll look forward to seeing you."

I stared at the letter through blurred vision in disbelief. I was touched by the fact that someone I had never met would be so thoughtful and sympathetic to my dilemma. I made plans to attend Mr. Rotcop's next workshop at Pierce College in Woodland Hills, California. I had never gone anywhere alone, but I was not going to let such a fantastic opportunity pass me by again.

My husband and I owned an old car at the time. One day he drove me to a local car dealership and bought me a brand new Honda Civic Sedan so that I would have reliable transportation on the long drive to Southern California. I owe everything to my husband, Darrell. He has been supportive of my writing career from the very beginning and continues to be to this day.

The Pitch

My screenwriting career began on a Thursday morning. I woke up early that day. Armed with the hand-drawn map that my husband had carefully made for me, I waved good-bye as I backed out of our driveway.

Heading south on Interstate 5 I felt an unbelievable pride in myself. I was taking a much-awaited step toward fulfilling my dream career. How I wished that my family could see me now. I could still hear them telling me, "You'll never amount to anything!" Yet, here I was, heading down to Los Angeles—alone, with only my dream. If my family could have seen me they would have been laughing.

Seven hours later I checked into a hotel only four blocks from Pierce College, where the screenwriting workshop would be held. I immediately called Mr. Rotcop, as he asked me to do when I arrived and we arranged to meet on campus the following morning before the workshop.

While sitting alone in the hotel room that night I began what was to become the first script I would ever sell, *Nowhere To Hide*.

In the morning I arrived at Pierce College an hour ahead of time. (I am always early.) Suddenly, I was face-to-face with thirty other wannabe screenwriters. I felt terrified. But after Mr. Rotcop introduced me to the group as his guest. my confidence was boosted somewhat.

Then, without warning, he asked the unthinkable of me: "Would you like to be first?"

At first I didn't have the slightest idea what he meant.

"Would you like to pitch your novel to the group?" He asked.

I looked from one face to another, then to Mr. Rotcop. I asked, "What's a pitch?"

He smiled and replied, "It's an oral synopsis of your story."

Fortunately, I knew the story like the back of my hand. I had lived it. It was about an event that had happened to me. I explained that it was my 350-page unpublished novel, *Vow of Vengeance.*

He looked into my eyes, "You don't have a problem speaking to the group, do you?"

After hesitating and searching for some sort of voice, I responded, "No. I guess not. It's just that . . . well, I'm a writer, not a public speaker."

Mr. Rotcop instantly responded, "If you're going to make it in this town, you've got to be both."

I will always remember that. In fact, nowadays when I'm asked to speak at conferences, I often have trouble keeping quiet.

I took a deep breath and, with all of the confidence I could muster, began my first Hollywood pitch. From the beginning, I felt as though everyone in the room, including Mr. Rotcop, was engrossed in my story. He had interest written all over his face, and I knew I had them—all of them.

As I completed my pitch, Mr. Rotcop walked over to me and said, "That's a commercial story. I think I can do something with it. You go home and write up the story you just told us as a screenplay and send it back down to me."

That's when I had to tell him that I had never even seen a screenplay. I had no idea what a script looked like.

Mr. Rotcop took a script out of his briefcase and handed it to me. He said, "Here, take this old script and use it as your guide. Put what we will see in the action. Make your dialogue sound as natural as you can. Make it real."

I have never forgotten those simple but essential guidelines for the screenwriting process. But, soon I would learn that the process was much harder to master than it sounded.

I never told Mr. Rotcop I didn't know what he meant by "a commercial script." Instead, I faked it and said, "No problem."

Driving North on Interstate 5 I was so preoccupied preparing my future Oscar acceptance speech that I completely missed my turnoff. I was halfway to San Francisco going in the wrong direction before I realized what I had done.

Six weeks later I had completed the first draft of *Vow of Vengeance*. I thought that was all I had to do. *Not so fast*.

All I had done was turn my 350-page novel into a 175-page script.

Submitting My First Script

Six weeks after my first introduction to the film industry I was sending my spec script to Mr. Rotcop at his request. Then I waited.

Two weeks later I found out how much of a roller-coaster ride this career was going to be. The producer was able to find a company who gave me an impressive writer's report (shown in it's entirety later in this chapter). They gave my first script a "yes," recommending it for production, along with the following advice: "You'll have to shorten the script because Hollywood doesn't do epics anymore."

Was it really going to be this easy? I was on my way—or so I thought.

In less than three weeks I received notification that the company had bellied up. My script was returned.

In the next section of this book, you will find excerpts from *Vow of Vengeance*. I hope you will learn from them. On these pages I am baring my soul by showing my rough talent at the beginning of my screenwriting career. The excerpts are from the first draft. Notice the blatant mistakes. Later I will show you how the full script was tightened to become the final draft which I sold.

Screenwriting is rewriting. But don't lose your story in the process—that's the soul of your script. Even the best formatted script needs soul.

My First Effort, My First Mistakes

(What I did and you shouldn't do!)

If your script looks anything like my following first draft, we have our work cut out for us. I want you to learn from my mistakes. Maybe this can save you time on your path.

The following is an excerpt of the first draft I submitted.

(title page)

VOW OF VENGEANCE

by

Andrea Leigh Wolf

Novel completed 12-13-86
First Draft Screenplay

Andrea Leigh Wolf
Street Address
City/State/Zip
Telephone Number

Pages 1-5 shown while credits are on screen:

Fade In:

INTERIOR/BAR/EVENING

The camera scans the smoke-filled bar. A grubby man, RALPH TILLSMAN, sits in one corner. His obese frame is wedged tightly in the captain's chair. A barmaid walks back and fourth serving other customers. Tillsman strains his eyes, trying to focus on the entrance. He drains the remaining beer from the bottle in one gulp. Tillsman BELCHES loudly, wiping the beer-suds from his beard.

TILLSMAN

What the hell ya
bastards looking at?

A loud CHUCKLE is heard from a scruffy man who has just entered the bar. He walks in Tillsman's direction.

PAUL

All I have to do is listen
and I can find you in a
crowded room.

Paul snickers as he seats himself at Tillsman's table.

                    TILLSMAN

                   (slurring)

          Where the hell you been?

                      PAUL

          (taking a drag on his cigarette)

              Now, calm your ass.

              I been looking to make

              a score. And you're gonna

              love what I found.

                    TILLSMAN

             (waving his arm,
                shouting to the barmaid)

              Oh yeah, well let's have
              another beer and we'll just see.
              Hey, we need a beer!

The barmaid saunters over to their table. She
stands a foot from their table. Her long stringy
hair atop her head at the beginning of the day,
has begun to fall to her shoulders. There are
dark circles beneath her eyes. She cracks her
gum as she arranges the ashtrays on her tray.

                    BARMAID

     Yeah, what you . . . gentlemen want?
     And, I use the term loosely.

Tillsman grabs her by the wrist. The barmaid
struggles to free herself.

                    BARMAID

     You're hurting me.

                    TILLSMAN

     Just shut your mouth and
     bring us both a beer.

                    BARMAID

     (blowing a huge bubble,
     rubbing her wrist)

     All right!

Tillsman waits until she is out of earshot and
slams his fist on the table.

                    TILLSMAN

     Sassy bitch! Now, what's
     the big fucking deal?

```
                    PAUL

                (chuckling)

        Here we go again.

                    PAUL

        No. I kid you not. This afternoon
        I went with my brother-in-law
        when he paid his rent. He lives
        in them apartments down from
        your place? The one with that
        chick you can't wait to get in
        her pants?
```

Well, you get the idea. Can you see the problems with formatting and the inconsistencies I had in this first effort? I am including these pages so you will see what NOT to do.

Now let's take a journey—the path of a spec script.

After completing my *Vow of Vengeance* script, I mailed it to Los Angeles. This first script was promptly returned to me. Afterwards, I used the following "Reader's Report" to completely rewrite the script. I want you to see the actual "Reader's Report" because it was such an eye-opener for me.

Reader's Report

The following Reader's Report was returned with my script, *Vow of Vengeance*. The Report (also known as "Coverage") is what happens to a script after it's submitted to a studio. I will use my own production company name here and not for confidentiality, the actual studio name .

CALLING CARD PRODUCTIONS

TITLE: VOW OF VENGEANCE   FORM: SCREENPLAY
AUTHOR: Andrea Leigh Wolf   PAGES: 175
LOCATION: Sacto/Florida   SUBMITTED BY: KR
GENRE: Dramatic Thriller   REVIEWED BY: SL
TIME: Present   RECEIVED: 5//23/88

RECOMMENDATION: __X__ yes _____ no _____ maybe

RALPH TILLSMAN vows to get back at a handful of people who put him behind bars for ten years. PAMELA RICHARDSON, who was the "major" person responsible for sending him to prison in the first place, is the last one left. And Tillsman is after her.

	Excellent	Good	Fair	Poor
Characterization	x			
Dialogue			x	
Structure			x	
Storytime	x			
Setting Prods Value		x		

Budget: _____ High _____ Medium __X__ Low

The following coverage was written by the studio's reader about my initial script.

By presenting this coverage here, I hope you will get a better idea of what a reader or story analyst is looking for when a script arrives at the production company.

SYNOPSIS:

JEFF and PAM RICHARDSON are a happily married couple. JEFF is a police officer. PAM manages an apartment complex in Sacramento in 1965. They live with their infant daughter, KIMBERLY.

Then, in one night, their peaceful existence is uprooted. TILLSMAN enters their lives. TILLSMAN knew PAM when she was in high school—although she has no memory of him. Over the years a lust for PAM has been building in the drugged and demonic mind of TILLSMAN. Finally, losing all sanity, TILLSMAN bursts into the apartment of the RICHARDSONS. Holding them hostage for more than three hours, TILLSMAN taunts PAM and JEFF. He threatens to kill them if they ever go to the police. Taking everything TILLSMAN can get his hands on, he leaves the house.

Not more than five hours later TILLSMAN is caught. He is convicted and sentenced to ten years behind bars. TILLSMAN wails he will get back at everyone. He will get out of jail and kill everyone involved in his conviction—especially PAM. No matter where she goes, no matter where she hides, he will find and kill her.

TILLSMAN may be in jail, PAM is still scared to death. Somehow she knows no prison walls will hold this man. He will not rest until she is dead.

As the months pass, TILLSMAN becomes a model prisoner. He does everything by the book, and after eighteen months he is up for parole.

Now TILLSMAN is out and on the war path. The first one killed is JEFF.

PAM goes into a wild panic. She knows it's TILLSMAN. RICHARD, JEFF'S partner, tells her to take it easy. They place a twenty-four hour watch on her and KIMBERLY.

RICHARD is in love with PAM. Although she cares deeply for RICHARD, PAM is not in love with him.

The terror of TILLSMAN showing up at any moment finally gets to PAM. Unable to take it any longer, she packs up and moves to a small town in Florida.

Meanwhile, RICHARD, and a team of detectives try desperately to track down TILLSMAN. It seems he lost a lot of weight in prison then had plastic surgery on his face after getting out.

PAM tries to get a new life started in Florida. She falls in love with MICHAEL, another police officer. He too puts twenty-four surveillance on her.

PAM begins working at a law office. One of the clerks, JONATHAN, acts suspiciously toward her. When she turns him down for a dinner date, he is almost hostile. A few days later—despite the surveillance, TILLSMAN bursts in on PAM and KIMBERLY. Sure enough, it's JONATHAN.

The final battle ensues. TILLSMAN has completely flipped his lid. He runs around like a man possessed.

MICHAEL bursts in on the scene. He and TILLSMAN lock in combat. And when it's over, MICHAEL lies wounded on the floor—and TILLSMAN lies in a body bag.

The previous synopsis is an exact copy of the Reader's Report on my screenplay—not my synopsis. I left the words as they were written. The studio reader presented a completely different spin on the story from what I had intended. I mention this because you must keep in mind that each person who reads your script may get a completely different feeling for both your writing and your story.

Having read the script, the reader then writes his or her own synopsis . . . .

The following is the reader's comments on that same script.

COMMENTS:

Some parts of this script are utterly wonderful. They're convincing, dramatic, frightening, and exhilarating. Other parts are dull, stupid, silly, and boring.

The parts that worked—really worked! The parts that didn't—really didn't!

TILLSMAN is a great villain. He's a character, not just a violent emotion. Every time we say, "He can't possibly get any worse," sure enough—he does.

I knew right away that JONATHAN was TILLSMAN in disguise.

I feel one thing is needed to tie the relationship between PAM and TILLSMAN together. There should be an incident from their past that caused this slow brewing hatred in TILLSMAN. Something had to cause him to feel she is a stuck-up bitch. It could be something as simple as PAM turning down TILLSMAN for a date. But there needs to be some common ground—some interesting point in both of their lives—that justifies TILLSMAN'S underlying hatred of PAM. Not only will this tie up loose ends, but it will make PAM and TILLSMAN stronger characters.

The biggest thing that didn't work for me was the relationship between PAM, RICHARD and MICHAEL.

I wanted to see PAM get together with RICHARD. The reason being: he's a developed character. I knew who he was. I never knew who MICHAEL was. He's just in there as a love interest. I found it a complete letdown that she and RICHARD didn't fall in love. If the author is going to give PAM to MICHAEL, MICHAEL must be a developed enough character that we feel it's justified. The audience must feel she made the right decision to go with him. Right now it's as if she's shortchanging herself and the audience. RICHARD is a great character. Michael is flat, one dimensional, and boring. There's no reason in the world for him and PAM to get together.

Another problem is with a lot of PAM'S lines. She spends half the time moaning and bemoaning how scared she is. It got to the point where it was so repetitious I wanted to scream, "Okay! I get the point. You're scared. I know! Now talk about something else!" But she doesn't. She just keeps going on about how petrified she is, and that somehow TILLSMAN is going to get her.

We have a strong female protagonist here, and that's a very popular ingredient in screenplays today. I felt she is strong enough to take care of TILLSMAN on her own. I think it would be much more dramatic and make PAM a much stronger character if she kills TILLSMAN. The way it's written now we have the typical damsel in distress being saved by the knight in shining armor.

Again, this could be justified if we made MICHAEL a stronger character.

As for the believability of the piece, it does seem a little far fetched at times. I find it amazing that TILLSMAN can kill fifteen people and not leave a clue.

Also, it tends to drag at times. The piece runs 175 pages! Although the pacing is fine, some nipping and tucking is needed.

The last flaw is the way the passage of time is handled. If it wasn't for the author telling me hours and days passed, I never would have known. This is most apparent in TILLSMAN'S first attack of JEFF and PAM. The attack seems to last five minutes (screen time). The screenplay says it takes three hours. Something's missing here.

With these problems taken care of, VOW OF VENGEANCE can work as a powerful dramatic thriller. A rewrite is definitely in order.

I used this reader's comments as a pattern by which to rewrite my script from page one. Although the film company never produced the project, I went on to option and later sell it.

A script can be rewritten over and over again. However, no amount of rewrites will work unless the story is strong.

The following are the opening pages of my revised screenplay, *Vow of Vengeance*, the draft that turned me from a "wannabe" screenwriter into a screenwriter who was paid for a script—15 rewrites later!

FADE IN:

INT. RICHARDSON'S APARTMENT - BEDROOM - NIGHT

JEFF RICHARDSON, 25, and his wife, PAM, 20, are making love. Their infant daughter, 6 months, KIMBERLY, sleeps in her crib a few feet away.

A framed LAW DEGREE hangs on the wall, reading PAMELA RICHARDSON. A freshly ironed HIGHWAY PATROL UNIFORM hangs on a hook on the wall.

Shattering the silence—a LOUD POUNDING from the front room. Pam jumps up. Jeff ignores it. The POUNDING continues.

                    JEFF
              Who the hell...

Jeff checks the clock.

                    JEFF (cont.)
              It's midnight for Christ sake!

Pam reaches for her robe. Jeff pulls her back.

                    JEFF (cont.)
              Not so fast. Maybe they'll
              go away.

Jeff kisses her. She MOANS with delight at his
touch. The POUNDING grows more urgent.

                    JEFF (cont.)
              It's probably one of the
              Andersons again.

The POUNDING is LOUDER.

                    PAM
              Don't they ever sleep?

                    JEFF
              They probably want me to settle
              one of their drunken brawls.

                    PAM
              Ooh—it's so hard being a
              big bad cop.

He kisses her as the POUNDING gets even louder.

                         28

                    PAM (cont.)
          You'd better answer it before
          they wake up the baby.

                    JEFF
          If she can sleep through a
          Rolling Stones concert, she
          can sleep through anything.

He grabs his Levi's hanging on the door. Puts
them on. Stumbles back to the bed, one leg
caught.

                    JEFF (cont.)
          You stay here.
          (Kissing her)
          Hold that thought.
He winks at her nakedness and leaves the room.

INT. LIVING ROOM - SAME

Jeff checks through the peep hole. Sees nothing.
Starts to go back to bed, and the POUNDING
resumes.

EXT. RICHARDSON'S APARTMENT - SAME

RALPH TILLSMAN, 25, three hundred pound, grubby
man waits in the dimly lit breezeway. His hair
and beard are long and unkempt. As the door
opens, the door-chain CLANKS.

INT. RICHARD'S APARTMENT - SAME
Jeff opens the door slightly. Tillsman steps
into view. SWAYS, obviously drunk.

                         JEFF
            What's your problem, buddy?

Tillsman doesn't answer. He KICKS the door
open, catching Jeff off balance. BREAKS the
chain and throws Jeff to the floor.

                    JEFF (cont.)
            What the...

Tillsman barges passed Jeff and into the apartment. Jeff grabs the intruder by the scruff of
the neck. Catches him off guard. Throws Tillsman
outside.
EXT. RICHARDSON'S APARTMENT - SAME

Tillsman sits stunned on the concrete walk
outside the door. Jeff grabs him, but Tillsman
suddenly draws a .45 automatic from the back
of his pants.

                    TILLSMAN
            All right, asshole! Get the
            fuck off me!

Jeff instantly raises both hands into the air.

   This is a good place to stop. You get the idea. Even now I
can see things I would do differently if I had it to do over,
which only proves that screenwriting is rewriting, and you
never stop learning.

Differences

The differences between my revised script and the first draft are obvious to me now. The format was corrected and the action is more direct. The dialogue is single-spaced. The only double spaces used are those that separate the action, the dialogue, or the slug lines. A slug line describes a change of scene using these abreviations: INT. (interior)/EXT. (exterior) – (LOCATION) – DAY/NIGHT), and that's it. It describes the scene direction, whether it's an interior or exterior scene, and whether it's day or night. Scripts with more information in the slug lines are shooting scripts. You are not writing a shooting script, but rather a spec script. Don't look like a novice by submitting a spec script with too much information in the slug lines.

Action paragraphs should never be more than four lines. Dialogue should be kept crisp. No rambling.

On My Own

Suddenly I was on my own—and had no idea where to market my spec script. How could I? I knew nothing about the film business except that I desperately wanted to be a part of it. I had come so close to selling my script the first time and now I wanted to sell it more than ever.

Clearly if I were going to have any sort of career in the industry I needed to make it happen for myself. No one was going to walk me down the yellow brick road of success and say, "Great script, kid! Here's a million dollars for your efforts. It'll be in theaters in three weeks."

So I began reading every book I could find about the film industry and screenwriting. I had heard real horror stories about writers getting bad agents and their careers being ruined before they were even started. I was determined to market myself. It never occurred to me to look for an agent. Besides, who would want to handle an unknown writer? Agents I had heard of would not have been interested in an unproven writer, and I didn't want an agent who was just starting out—a newbe, like me. That would be like the blind leading the blind. I decided I'd stay on my own and learn by trial and error.

Most of all I wanted to know who was reading my scripts at any given time. I had learned that if you send your script to a particular production company they can make copies of your script and send it to other readers without your ever knowing. I have learned a lot by working for myself.

I know unproven screenwriters who are holding out for six-figure sales to major studios. Yet they should look at the situation realistically. They need to build a résumé and gain experience. They need to learn their craft and work hard.

I've met a few writers who began when I did. They chose to find an agent first. Nine years later they are still looking for that agent and they have never written another script.

Life is too short to waste so much time while your dream goes unfulfilled. There is another way.

After reading almost every film industry book, I began reading the trades from cover to cover. I had to find a strategy.

I went to Los Angeles as often as possible to attend screenwriters' conferences and seminars. I spent money that I didn't have because my writing was important to me.

It was also essential for me to meet people in this business, to network. Actually, the networking appeals to me most of all. It's as much fun as the writing.

Exposure to industry insiders was like a narcotic—the more people I met, the more I wanted to meet. Just being around them made me feel as if I could really be a screenwriter!

I've always believed that if you surround yourself with successful people, you will eventually learn from them. I have also loved the challenge of marketing my own work.

From day one I kept a journal of the path that I have traveled to the successful first sale of my script. In fact, I have continued to keep a journal to this day.

A journal can provide information you may need to refer to later. For example, you may need a reminder about when and where you sent your script and to whom.

In May 1988 I began actively marketing my script on my own. I had heard that a San Francisco Bay Area writer's group was hosting a luncheon meeting. Their scheduled guest speaker was an independent producer. Immediately, I sent a note to the Club's president to find out if the producer was accepting new material. She called a few days later and said, "Yes!" She had spoken with the producer, and he had asked to see my script before the meeting the following week. Not wanting to waste a second, I mailed the script that afternoon.

That following Saturday I woke up early and drove to San Francisco. I was early as usual. I sat waiting and wondering if I would sell my script that day.

As I walked into the room my heart was pounding so hard I could barely hear anything else. I sat at a table and began talking to the other writers as we waited for lunch. Suddenly the producer bent down and whispered in my ear, "My executive producer is flying in from Canada to speak to you about your project, *Vow of Vengeance*. He'll be here later this afternoon."

I don't remember much of what he said after, "My executive producer is flying in from Canada . . . ." The ladies sitting near me had heard the news and began congratulating me.

Later that day the producer and I drove to a nearby restaurant to meet with the executive producer. I sat between the two men; one was dressed very expensively, the other was not. They ordered dinner. I was too excited to eat so I ordered only a soda. We discussed my plans for *Vow of Vengeance*—who I imagined in the leading roles, etc. (Boy, was I green.)

At one point, the Canadian producer asked, "How much do you want for your script? Do you want to be 'associate producer'?"

Instantly I knew I was in way over my head. I wondered, what the heck am I doing here? Being new to this field, I was afraid of being the associate producer. I thought I'd be expected to help fund the project. Dumb, right?

He began talking purchase price for my script. "I'll give you $50,000—but no more," he said. "This is your first script, that's as high as I'll go."

I agreed to that price as the other producer returned to the table. The Canadian asked if the other producer had a copy of my script. He said he did. We all walked out of the restaurant.

The Canadian producer explained, "It's too late for my bank to cut a check of that size. I'll have to wait until Monday morning. Will that be okay?"

I agreed.

They asked me to drive the Canadian producer to the San Francisco Airport and I agreed to that as well. Then I drove the other producer to his home in Hillsboro, a wealthy community south of the San Francisco Airport.

All the way home I was so anxious to tell my husband the great news that I took several exits off the freeway to try to call home. But our teenager was on the phone and the line was busy. (This was before *Call Waiting*™.)

To my surprise, I never heard from either of those producers again. I had been scammed. When I finally contacted the producer he denied everything.

The moral of this story is this: there are many honest, legitimate people out there, and then there are the types I met with that day in San Francisco. You have to be aware that there are many sharks swimming in the industry waters! Never rely on anything that isn't in writing.

There I was alone that day, driving around with two men I had never met before. What was I thinking?

This shows how vulnerable you can be when you're too eager to sell your screenplay.

Next came the Italy deal that almost was.

A few weeks after the San Francisco incident, I looked through the "Scripts Wanted" section of *Variety*. The Five Rooms Production Company in Milan, Italy, was looking for scripts. You guessed it! I sent off *Vow of Vengeance*. About two weeks later, at 5:30 a.m. on a Sunday morning, the phone rang. It was Alberto Cinicola, the Head of the Five Rooms Production Company, I heard his delightful, heavy Italian accent dimly across the miles.

He asked, "Do you have a fax number? We loved your script. We'd like to fax our contract."

I did not have my own fax machine at the time so I gave him the fax number of a local office supply business.

(Tip: If you don't have your own fax machine, always have handy the fax of a nearby business who accepts faxes.)

Mr. Cinicola said, "Read over the contract and I will call you later today."

I couldn't wait to get dressed, get down to the store, and pick up the fax from Italy. Unfortunately, I had to wait until 10 a.m. for the store to open since it was Sunday, but when I received the contract it was fantastic. They wanted me to fly to Milan to work with another screenwriter on a specific project. They offered to provide First Class airfare and accommodations. They would also pay for all of my living expenses during my stay.

They wanted to know what I wanted as a weekly salary. I had no idea so a friend of mine gave me the name of her agent and I called him. He told me to ask $2,500 per week and $10,000 up front for my travel expenses.

I relayed this request to Mr. Cinicola when he called. And just as quickly, the deal was off. It was too much money for his small company.

I contacted the agent again who chuckled and said, "Of course it was too much! They were supposed to negotiate!"

The funny thing was, no one had told the Italians they were supposed to negotiate. And no one had told *me* they were supposed to negotiate—until it was too late.

I lost a dream deal for a new writer because I had relied on an agent who had no stake in the outcome of that deal. Another hard lesson learned . . . but who's counting?

I made several calls to Italy to try to get the deal going again but they had already decided against it. I was devastated—and back to square one.

It would be another year, and more than five "page-one-rewrites" (a page-one-rewrite is when you rewrite a script from the first page), before I would finally option my script to a production company in Vermont.

As with the Italian deal, I found the Vermont Entertainment company's "Call For Scripts" in the

Hollywood Reporter. Again I mailed my script to the address listed in the ad. As before, the company loved the script and called me. They were very interested in producing the script. They called often but then there was a slight problem. They wanted to know if I would mind rewriting a funeral scene to be shot in the small Vermont town of Rutland.

"No problem," I responded.

The funding was coming in at a rapid pace but the producer was growing more intent on acting in the film.

I began to worry. First, the company was backing him as a producer, not an actor. Also there was no part in the film for him. And then he wanted to direct.

Suddenly, one by one, the backers began to withdraw their funding.

Five months later the producers were in Los Angeles to receive an award. I agreed to meet with them there. We got together three days after I arrived. The meeting with the producer and his assistant producer lasted a few hours.

Four months later the project got the red light. The producer/actor and finally the director had been dropped by the Entertainment Company. Again, my script was returned to me.

Marketing

Marketing is a huge part of the screenwriting process. Writing the spec script is just the beginning, the tip of the iceberg. It is the actual marketing of the script that takes its toll on so many new screenwriters. The marketing process can damage your psyche. However, it can be done successfully—without an agent.

The previous deals had fallen through, but I had learned from them. From the beginning I have kept two books close at hand. Both are written by Mark Litwak, a highly acclaimed entertainment attorney. These two books are a must if you intend to go it alone.

1) *Reel Power: The Struggle for Influence
    and Success in the New Hollywood*
    Silman James Press, 1993

2) *Deal-Making in the Film & Television Industry:
    From Negotiations to Final Contract*
    Silman James Press, 1998

These two books are, in my opinion, among the most valuable to every new and seasoned screenwriter. I have referred to them many times along my journey.

You must wear many hats on your journey. You will have to be an agent, a business manager, a public relations person, and more. Most of all, you must keep your various hats on straight.

In Hollywood, you are only as good as your last success. The struggle never ends, so as a new writer you must hustle more and write better than the established screenwriters.

I suggest that you map out your path and then stick to it. This reminds me of the famous lines in the film *Pretty Woman*, "Do you have a goal? You have to have a goal."

And it reminds me of the expression, "The only rule is that there are no rules." Do whatever works for you.

The Business of Screenwriting

Your first priority is to learn the business of screenwriting. Learn the language of Hollywood. Be creative. Do whatever you can to promote your work. Allow your excitement to fill your aura. If you're excited about your script, it will excite industry people. It's catching!

As I mentioned earlier—and I can't stress this enough—be ready to pitch your script to anyone! You never know to whom you are *really* talking. The person could be a scout for Steven Spielberg. People who can get your script produced do not wear neon signs.

Right after I optioned my first screenplay, people who had completed a script of their own and did not know what to do with it began to approach me. They'd ask, "How did you know where to send your script? How did you know what type of script the independent producers wanted?"

When you believe that your script is the best it can be, register it with the WGA. If you live West of the Mississippi, register it with the WGA, West. If you live East of the Mississippi, register it with the WGA, East. Then mail the script. A script will not sell if you keep it hidden in your desk drawer!

You have to be relentless. Don't get discouraged. You'll need the skin of an armadillo and a bottle of good Chardonnay. At first there may be many rejections, so be prepared. Even after you have sold a script there will be rejections. It's part of the process, part of the game. If you're lucky, the rejections become more encouraging. Then, finally, the phone rings!

Remember, there are many sharks swimming in the Hollywood waters. But keep in mind, not all sharks bite. Besides, there's always shark repellent!

With my first failures behind me and the realization that I was alone, I had a stiff drink, a good cry, and dug my heels in for the long haul. My first word processor had to go. In its place my husband bought me a new personal computer, a letter-quality printer, and a fax machine.

Being a screenwriter is a business. You have made the decision to write for money. As a business owner you will need some understanding of the film industry. You need to learn marketing skills. Otherwise, you will be at a great disadvantage. If you wait until you get a nibble on your script, it may be too late. When someone shows an interest in your script it's easy to be flattered so you may make mistakes.

Many of the people with whom you may be dealing will know the movie business well. If you know it too, no one will be able to take advantage of you. So do your homework. You can't sell your screenplay unless you know enough about the film business to plan a marketing strategy. You must know who the players are and they are changing all the time. Hollywood is one big food chain with everyone feeding off one another. There is nothing wrong with that. It's just a fact. Your job is to get your script as far up the food chain as possible.

To create a successful plan read every book on screenwriting that you can. Attend festivals and conferences. Keep up with current news about Hollywood, whether or not you live there. Do this by reading the trades such as *Variety*, *The Hollywood Reporter*, *Fade In*, *Written By*, and *Drama-Logue*—a few of the best sources.

Learn Hollywood jargon so you can use it when appropriate and understand it when it's used by others. In this book's Glossary I have defined some industry terms to get you started.

Continue writing after you send out your script. Go to as many current films as possible. Seeing the latest releases shows you what's selling in Hollywood and beyond.

Make contacts. Network on the Internet. There are hundreds of screenwriting websites. In the back of this book is a list of websites that are beneficial to screenwriters.

Meeting Hollywood Insiders
Outside of Hollywood

If you don't live in Hollywood, let Hollywood come to you. And if you want industry people to take you seriously, you're going to have to take yourself and your talent seriously.

Every year hundreds of writers' conferences, seminars, and film festivals are held all over the world. Speakers come from the Hollywood community, such as insiders like J. Kenneth Rotcop (mentioned before) who helped me a lot.

Most of the speakers are insiders with various degrees of success. Some are only just starting out and have more recent credits, while others have credits from the early days of TV. But all have experience from which you can learn.

I have been a speaker at several conferences and I find these events stimulating. It's informative to hear from other speakers and the many up-and-coming screenwriters.

Some film industry insiders accept such speaking engagements in order to search for "diamonds in the rough." They make themselves available to conference attendees. They are willing to talk and listen to you at this time so take advantage of this tremendous opportunity. It's a great way for beginning writers to make contacts.

When I'm a guest speaker at a conference I enjoy talking to all kinds of screenwriters—from the beginners to the more experienced ones. As speakers we agree to make ourselves available to the attendees. I always take about 500 business cards and brochures to hand out so that people can get in touch with me later.

I suggest that you create your own professional business cards to help launch your writing career. Tearing off small pieces of paper on which to write your phone number and address looks tacky and unprofessional. Exchange cards with others at conferences, seminars, and events. Then follow through by contacting them while they still remember you.

It's disappointing to give out my business cards and not receive any in exchange. I still have all the cards that were given to me at the conferences I attended early in my career.

Keep an organized collection of the business cards you receive. Alphabetize them or arrange them according to job categories (directors, producers, writers, etc.).

When you attend conferences and seminars ask for business cards from the speakers. Most will be happy to provide them. This is how you build your networking skills. Some speakers will maintain contact with you, some will not. I'm still in touch with many writers I've met along the way. I love to hear how they're doing with their work.

Never go to a conference without something to pitch. You never know who you'll meet. Take your completed script and leave it in your room, just in case. Being prepared will impress the speaker or other industry person who might ask to see your work. You will appear to be a more professional and serious screenwriter. If you don't have anything ready you should at least make a contact for later when your work is ready for review.

Never say, "I have a great idea! I just need someone to write the script." And don't ask, "Can't I just sell my idea?" There are literally thousands, if not millions, of people around Hollywood with fantastic "ideas." What industry insiders want to see are completed scripts.

Be positive. Never say, "I don't like ____ (a particular director, producer, actor, etc.)." Negative remarks may come back to bite you.

Finally, never hand speakers your script unless they ask for it. The speakers will usually not accept it anyway. I don't take unsolicited scripts. If the speakers do take your script they may leave it behind unless they are truly interested in it. If they are actively seeking talent they will let you know. You don't want to appear pushy but you want to be ready.

Never miss the social functions at conferences and seminars. This is the best time for you to network. When events are held at hotels make sure you get a room there or close by. Go to the meetings every day and attend all the functions you can so you won't miss anything.

One of the most stimulating conferences I ever attended was, "The Art and Business of Screenwriting." Held in 1993 in New York City, it was sponsored by the Independent Film Project (IFP) and the WGA, East.

The speaker lineup was incredible and well worth the cost of attendance. It was the farthest I had ever traveled for a conference. Even though it was on the East Coast I was determined to attend it. The following is a reproduction of their program.

Classes and Speakers at the New York Conference

Day One

"Writing for Low-Budget Indies" ("Indies" are independently-produced films or shows) with:
  Jan Oxenberg, Producer, Red Wagon Productions
  Tony Chan, Writer/Director/Producer, *Combination Platter*
  Leslie Harris, Writer/Director, *Just Another Girl on the IRT*
  Ted Hope, Line Producer, *The Unbelievable Truth*
  Tom Kalin, Writer/Director/Producer, *Swoon*
  Christine Vachon, Producer, *Swoon*

"Writing and Rewriting *Mad Dog* and *Glory*" with Richard Price! It was set it up like an interview by Alice Arlen, Screenwriter of *Silkwood* and *Cookie*.

Lunch break

"Ask an Agent" with moderator, Janet Roach, Screenwriter, *Prizzi's Honor*. Agents in attendance included:
 Wiley Hausam, ICM
 David J. Kanter, United Talent Agency
 Sterling Lord, President, Sterling Lord Literistic,
 Scott Yoselow, The Gersh Agency

"Pitching Your Project"
Attendees (about 300) worked together in small groups of about 75 people for a practical workshop on pitching their projects. Before the conference they drew three names from the attendees and I was chosen to pitch. We pitched to these industry insiders:
 Grace Blake, Associate Producer, *Silence of the Lambs*
 Elizabeth Carroll, Director of Development, Vanguard Films
 Lynn Holst, V.P. of Creative Affairs, American Playhouse
 Susan Kougvell, Co-Chairperson, Su-City Picture
 Roseanne Leto, Senior V.P. of Development, Laurel Entertainment
 Bruce Weiss, President/Producer, Cornerstone Films

Reception

Day Two

"Are We There Yet?"
At what point does the writing process end and the revision process begin? with:
 Susan Kouguell and Susan Slonaker, Su-City Pictures

"Optioning Your Script"
A discussion of some legal aspects of optioning a property: obtaining the rights to a novel, play, short

story, or other existing work. What to expect when you are asked to do a rewrite. The differences between a revision and a rewrite. Moderated by Steven Starr, Writer/Director of *Joey Breaker*. Panelists included:

Janet Grillo, Senior V.P. of Production, New Line Cinema

Rosalind Lichter, Esq., Chasen & Lichter

Amos Poe, Screenwriter, *Rocket Gibraltar*

Monty Ross, Producer, *Malcom X*

John Sloss, Esq., Sloss Law Office, P.C.

John Williams, President, Vanguard Films

May Withrick, V.P. of Development, Tribecca Prods.

"Meet the Development Executive— Find out what development executives are looking for" with:

Caroline Andoscia, East Coast Director, Scott Rubin Productions

Lynn Holst, V.P. Creative Affairs, American Playhouse

David Linde, Senior V.P. Sales & Acquisitions, Miramax International

Susan Margolin, Executive V.P. C.O.O. New Video Group

Ruth Pomerance, V.P. Lee Rich Productions

(Author Note: The N.Y. Conference saved the best for last...)

"Adaptation From Another Medium"
During an in-depth interview, Aaron Sorkin discussed adapting his award-winning Broadway hit "A Few Good Men" for the screen. Facilitator: Don Scardino, Artistic, Director, Playwrights Horizons.

(Author Note: I 've included this conference program to give you an idea of the various talent you may meet at conferences and to encourage you to attend various events.)

When You Option A Script

Two weeks after I returned from the New York Conference I optioned my script, *Vow Of Vengeance*. I am enclosing a copy of that option agreement to familiarize you with one of the various types of contracts you may encounter. Option agreements are rarely the same. They can be as simple as a few lines or as lengthy as the one that follows. It depends on the individual producer's wishes.

Even if you do not have an agent, you may want to hire an entertainment attorney to look over your contracts. But if you know what options are available to you, you may be able to negotiate your own contracts. Only you know what is best for *you*. Writers must make their own decisions about this. At least getting an option is one step closer to a successful writing career.

The following agreement was not the best one I could have received but it was the one I chose to sign. After all, a credit is a credit. I hope sharing this sample option agreement will be helpful to you, the potential or beginning screenwriter.

OPTION AGREEMENT

This Option Agreement (The "Option Agreement") made as of this _____ day of_____, _____ by and between _____ (hereafter "Artist"), and _____ (hereafter Production Company), and _____ (hereafter "Producer").

Recitals

WHEREAS, Artist has written and owns all rights in and to the original story and screenplay entitled _____ (collectively, the "Work"); and

WHEREAS, Artist desires to grant and Producer desires to accept an option to purchase any and all rights with respect to the Work under the terms and conditions of this Option Agreement.

NOW THEREFORE, in consideration of the mutual promises contained herein, the receipt and sufficiency of which is hereby acknowledged, the parties hereby agree as follows:

1. OPTION. In consideration of the payment to the Artist of the sum of (this can be anywhere from $1.00 to one-third of the purchase price if sold)—(the "Exercise Price"), payment of which shall be concurrent with the execution hereof, Artist hereby grants Producer the exclusive, irrevocable rights and option (hereinafter the "Option") to purchase any and all rights in and to the Work (hereafter the "Rights"), which Rights are further enumerated in reference herein (the "Assignment").

2. TERM OF OPTION. The Option may be exercised by Producer at any time during the twelve (12) month period commencing on the date hereof (the "Initial Term").

3. EXERCISE OF OPTION. Producer may exercise the Option to purchase the Rights by giving Artist written notice of Producer's election to exercise such Option (the "Exercise Notice"), which notice shall acknowledge and reaffirm Producer's obligation to pay to Artist

an aggregate amount equal to _____ dollars ($_____), payable as follows: fifty percent (50%) of the purchase price upon commencement of Pre-production, and 50% of the purchase price upon commencement of Principal photography of the Picture.

Note: This is not part of the agreement. I want to explain that if I were offered this agreement today, knowing what I know now, I would not have signed it. The reason is that if the project falls by the wayside, Pre-production may never happen. Then I would have been out of luck. I would have received no money, yet I would have sold rights to my script. I want to show you these steps and just how far down "Pre-production" ranks:

Step 1. Acquisition
Step 2. Development
Step 3. Packaging
Step 4. Production financing
Step 5. Pre-production

Therefore, your script would have to make it through the first four steps before you would receive a single cent. Back then I was unaware of this important detail when I signed this agreement. I could have been burned. This subject is covered in more detail later. The more information you have, the more you can avoid some of the mistakes I've made.

Now back to the Option Agreement . . .

4. EXECUTION AND DELIVERY OF AGREEMENT. Concurrently with the execution of the Option Agreement, Artist has executed and deposited with Producer the Assignment in the form of Exhibit B and the Rights Acquisition and Services Agreement ("The Rights Agreement") in the form of Exhibit A, both attached hereto. This Option Agreement and the Assignment and Rights Agreement shall be deemed dated as of the effective date of such Exercise Notice, they shall be deemed fully and validly executed and delivered as of such date. As soon thereafter as is practicable, Artist shall deliver to Producer any and all documents or Instruments of transfer reasonably requested by Producer to effectuate and validly transfer all rights in and to the Work to Producer pursuant to the terms hereof, specifically the Rights Agreement, provided, however, that the failure of the parties to do so shall not affect the validity of the Option Agreement or the Assignment. If Producer shall fail to exercise the Option, the Assignment, and Rights Agreement, it shall, upon the expiration of the Term of the Option, be of no further force or effect and Producer shall mark the Assignment "void."

5. REPRESENTATION, WARRANTIES and COVENANTS.

(A) Artist hereby warrants, represents and covenants that as of the date hereof and, if the Option is exercised, at all times prior to the date the Rights are transferred pursuant to the Assignment and the Rights Agreement and this Option Agreement, or otherwise throughout the Term, the following representations and warranties are and shall remain true and correct: Artist is the sole owner of the Work and has the full right and authority to enter into this agreement and to convey the Rights herein granted. The Work is wholly original in all respects and no part thereof is taken from any other literary material. The use by Producer of any Rights will not defame, libel or slander any person, or infringe upon any other rights of any party whatsoever. The Work has not previously been exploited in any medium. The Work is protected by copyright in the United States and in all countries adhering to the Universal Copyright Convention, and Artist has not therefore sold, assigned, encumbered or impaired any of the right, title or interest in and to the Work.

    (B) Artist hereby indemnifies and agrees to hold Producer, its officers, shareholders, employees, successors and assigns, under obligation, expense, lien, action, and cause of action (including the payment of reasonable attorney's fees costs actually incurred, whether or not in connection with litigation) based on, in connection with, or arising out of any breach by Artist on any warranties, representations or covenants contained herein or incorporated herein by indemnification to survive the Term of this Option Agreement.

    (C) During the Term, Artist shall not engage in any act or make any statement which is in conflict with, inconsistent with, or in derogation of any of the rights granted herein in the Assignment.

(6) NO OBLIGATION TO PRODUCE. Nothing herein shall be constructed to obligate Producer to produce, distribute, release or exhibit any Picture or to otherwise exploit any of the Rights granted Producer herein.

(7) ASSIGNMENT. Producer shall have the right, in its sole discretion, to assign its Rights hereunder. In the event of any such assignment, reference to, and provision relating to Producer herein and in the Assignment, he or she shall be deemed to refer to and relate to Producer's assignee to the extent, and subject to any limitation of such assignment.

(8) FURTHER INSTRUMENTS. Artist agrees to duly execute, acknowledge, and deliver to Producer or procure the due execution, acknowledgment, and delivery to Producer, of any and all further assignments and other instruments, in form approved by counsel for Producer, necessary or desirable to carry out and effectuate and deliver or cause to be so executed and delivered any such assignment or other instrument. Producer shall be deemed to be, and Artist hereby irrevocably appoints Producer, the true and lawful attorney-in-fact or Artist, with full right substitution and delegation, to execute and deliver in the name of the Artist or otherwise any and all such assignments and other instruments and to do any and all acts and things reasonably required to effectuate the purposes of this Option Agreement and the Assignment.

(9) GOVERNING LAW. This Agreement shall in all respects be governed and controlled by the laws of the state of California.

(10) NO REFUND OR CREDIT. The Option Price paid to Artist hereunder shall not be refunded to Producer in the event the Option is not exercised.

(11) NOTICES. All notices, requests, demands, and other communications hereunder shall be in writing and shall be made by mail (postage prepaid) return receipt requested or by reputable air courier, to the addresses herein designated in writing by notice given in the manner provided herein, and shall be deemed effective on the date personally delivered, or telefaxed, 48 hours following deposit in the U.S. mail, whether or not delivery is accepted and one day after deposit with air courier:

If to Producer: (address/name of Producer).
If to Artist: (address/name of Artist).

(12) ENTIRE AGREEMENT. This Option Agreement, including the provisions incorporated herein by reference, and the exhibits attached hereto, constitutes the entire agreement between the parties and cannot be modified except by written instrument executed and delivered by Producer and Artist. This Option Agreement supersedes all prior agreements without any limitations whatsoever, made between the parties. Neither Producer nor Artist has made any representations, warranties or promises which are not set forth herein or in any exhibit hereto. Each of the parties acknowledges that this Option Agreement has been executed only in reliance on representations, warranties and promises set forth herein.

(13) MORE FORMAL AGREEMENT. Upon exercise of the Option, it is contemplated that a more

formal rights acquisition agreement may be prepared containing the terms set forth herein and such standard terms as are customary in the motion picture industry in agreements of this nature and as may be agreed to by the parties. Until and unless such formal agreement is executed, this agreement, the Assignment and the Rights Agreement shall constitute the entire understanding and agreement of the parties hereto.

   IN WITNESS WHEREOF, the parties hereto have caused this agreement to be dully executed and delivered the day and year above written.

PRODUCER:_____

ARTIST:_____

Exhibit B

ASSIGNMENT

Reference is hereby made to that certain Option Agreement date as of _____(the "Option Agreement") and between _____ (Production Company), _____ ("Producer") and _____ ("Artist"). In connection therewith, Producer and Artist acknowledge and agree that the effective date of his assignment shall be the date Producer delivers to Artist the Exercise Notice as defined in and pursuant to the terms of the Agreement.

   In consideration of all payment made by Producer to Artist pursuant to the terms of the Agreement, and other good and valuable consideration, the receipt and sufficiency of which, the Artist hereby grants, sells, assigns, and transfers to Producer, its successor and assigns:

1. All of her exclusive worldwide rights in and to (i) the screenplay entitled _____ hereinafter, the "Screenplay" (ii) the original story and screenplay upon which such screenplay is based, (iii) all story, characters and other literary rights relating to such original story, screenplays and the screenplay, (iv) the episodes, characters and plots contained therein, (v) all rights in and to all subsequent revisions of such story, screenplays, and the screenplay, (vi) all outlines, notes, screenplay material and other such materials which were and may be used to develop and produce a theatrical motion picture project based on the screenplay, which materials shall include the title, characters, plot, motive and other elements thereof, and (vii) all manners of exploitation of the screenplay and the story incidents embodied in such a story and such screenplay, and any patents, trademarks, trade names or other similar rights and all sequel, remake, television series, and merchandising rights.

2. Any and all causes of action which Artist now or hereafter may have for any past, present or future infringement or interference with any of the rights granted to Producer in Paragraph 1, above.

Artist hereby irrevocably appoints Producer, its successor and assigns as her attorney with full power of substitution and delegation in Artist's name to enforce and protect all rights granted thereunder or any rights derivable therefore; to prevent or terminate any infringement or threatened violate or said rights; and to litigate, collect and receive all damages arising from any such suit or proceeding, as Producer my determine in its sole discretion.

IN WITNESS WHEREOF, each of the undersigned has executed this Assignment this _____ day of _____, _____.

Accepted and Acknowledged this____day of_____, _____.

By:_____ SS#_____.
By:_____ SS#_____.
City:_____
COUNTY of:_____
STATE of:_____

On this_____day of_____, _____ (year), before me_____ personally appeared _____, known to me to be the person executing this assignment on his or her own behalf.

_____
(NOTARY PUBLIC)

RIGHTS ACQUISITION AND SERVICE AGREEMENT

Reference is hereby made to that certain Option Agreement dated as of _____, _____. (The "Agreement") and _____ ("Artist"). In connection therewith, Producer and Artist acknowledge and agree that the effective date of this Rights Acquisition Agreement shall be the date Producer delivers to Artist the Exercise Notice as defined in and pursuant to the terms of the Agreement.

RECITALS

A. Artist and Producer have heretofore entered into agreement whereby for payment to Artist of ($_____) AMOUNT (the "Option Price"), Producer was granted an option (the "Option"), as defined in Item 2 on Page 1 of the Option Agreement, to purchase all of Artist's rights, title and interest in and to an original screenplay written by Artist and owned by Artist and currently entitled, _____ (hereinafter, the "Screenplay"). The Screenplay, the original story and any subsequent revisions thereto, and the episodes and characters contained therein, and all manners of exploitation of the story, and the screenplay described above, and the media throughout the universe in perpetuity, are hereinafter collectively referred to as the "Work".

B. Producer now desires to exercise such Option to purchase all of Artist's rights in and to the Screenplay and the Work on the terms and conditions set forth herein and to produce a feature length motion picture based upon the Screenplay and the Work (the "Picture") and to exploit such Picture in all manners and media throughout the universe.

C. Artist desires to grant and assign to Producer all of her collective rights in and to the Screenplay and Work, and to consummate

56

and the Work pursuant to the terms and conditions set forth herein.

NOW THEREFORE, in consideration of the foregoing and of the mutual covenants and promises set forth herein, the parties agree as follows:

AGREEMENT

1. GRANT OF RIGHTS AND ASSIGNMENTS. In consideration of the covenants of Producer set forth herein and in light of the rights of Producer under the Option Agreement, Artist hereby exclusively grants, sells, assigns, and transfers to Producer all of his or her collective rights of any kind or nature in and to the Screenplay and the Work including, without limitation, the exclusive worldwide rights included in the definition of the Work set forth in Recitals A above (collectively, the "Rights"). Concurrently with the execution hereof, Artist is executing and delivering to Producer a short-form assignment in the form attached to the Agreement as assignment set forth in this section I. Artist further grants biographical information relating to Artist in connection with publicizing, promoting and marketing the Picture and the Producer's rights therein.

2. CONSIDERATION.

(A) Consideration of Rights. Producer shall pay to Artist the aggregate amounts set forth below in full consideration of the Rights granted to Producer by Artist pursuant to Section I herein.

(i) Fixed Compensation. Artist hereby acknowledges and agrees that upon execution hereof, he or she shall be deemed to have received appropriate notice of Producer's election to exercise its Option and that in consideration of Rights granted to Producer who shall pay to Artist an aggregate sum of $_____ (purchase price) as follows: 50% upon start of pre-production and 50% upon start of principal photography of the Picture.

(ii) Obligation of Producer. Producer and Artist are independent contractors, Artist shall at no time during the term hereof be deemed an employee of Producer. Artist shall be solely responsible for the performance of all obligations in connection with Artist's service hereunder including, but not limited to, all wages, salaries, Social Security, Unemployment, Workman's Compensation and State Disability Insurance payments, and Artist shall be solely responsible for the payment of all union dues, federal, state, and local taxes, and other payroll deduction items, and for the satisfaction of the requirements of federal, state, and local laws.

3. Credits.

Writer's Credits. Artist shall receive credits in connection with the Picture in accordance with and to the minimum extent required by the Writers Guild of America's Basic Agreement. Producer shall determine, in its sole discretion, the size, style, manner and placement of such credits.

4. Representations, Warrants, and Covenants of Artist. The Artist hereby represents and warrants as follows, provided, however, that

all of the covenants, representations and warranties in Subsections 6 (b) and 6 (c) as they relate to the Screenplay shall be to the best of Artist's knowledge:

(a) No Conflict or Consent. Artist has full right and authority to enter into this Agreement and is not subject to any agreement or understanding relating to the work, the Screenplay, or otherwise, which could or might conflict with the terms hereof or prevent or hinder Producer's full use and quiet enjoyment of the rights granted to Producer herein. None of the rights conveyed to Producer herein have in any way been used, exploited, granted or otherwise disposed of, limited or impaired, and the same are free and clear of any and all liens or claims whatsoever.

(b) Ownership of Rights. As between Artist on one hand and Producer on the other, upon execution of the Agreement, Producer will own all rights in and to the Work and the Screenplay whether now known or existing or hereafter developed, in perpetuity throughout the universe.

(c) Infringement. The Screenplay and the Work are Artist's original works or are comprised of materials owned and controlled by Artist including, without limitation, the original story written by Artist and, except for scenes, dialogue, or characters added to Screenplay, the Work by Producer in connection with the production of the Picture based upon the Screenplay, the Work will in no way infringe upon the copyright, proprietary rights, or other personal rights of any person or entity and the production and exhibition of the Picture will not result in a claim by any party of invasion or infringement of personal, publicity, or proprietary rights of such party, unfair competition, libel, slander, defamation, or any similar claims.

(d) Claims. There are no claims or litigation pending, outstanding or threatened, adversely affecting or which may in any way prejudice Artist's or Producer's rights in the Screenplay, or the copyright or any title thereof or any of the rights conveyed herein and Artist has no reason to believe in the existence of any such claims.

5. COPYRIGHTS. Producer shall have the exclusive right to secure copyright and/or trademark registration and any renewals or extensions thereof (or equivalent protection in countries where no copyright or trademark law exists) of the Work, including the Screenplay. To the extent the Work has been validly copyrighted and/or registered for copyright in the United States of America, Producer shall be deemed to have acquired and is hereby granted and assigned all rights under any such copyright and/or trademark and, if requested by Producer, Artist agrees to execute, acknowledge and deliver, or cause to be executed, acknowledged and delivered, to Producer any instrument that may be required by Producer to establish and vest in Producer such rights.

6. INDEMNIFICATION.

(a) Producer's Indemnification. Producer agrees to indemnify and fully hold harmless Artist, his or her agents, successors and permitted assigns from and against any and all losses, damages, liabilities, obligations, judgments, settlements, costs and other expenses incurred or suffered by any of them, whether during or after the term upon or related to (i) the breach by Producer or any of its representations, warranties or covenants hereunder, (ii) any material added to the Screenplay by Producer or (iii) the development, production or exploitation of Picture, except such losses, damages, liabilities, obligations, judgments, settlements, costs, or expenses for which Artist shall be obligated to indemnify Producer pursuant to Section 6(b) hereof.

(b) Artist's Indemnification. Artist hereby agrees to indemnify fully and hold harmless Producer, any parent corporation, subsidiaries or affiliates of Producer and the respective officers, directors, shareholders, employees, agents, successors and assigns of Producer and all such other entitled (hereinafter "Producer's Indemnified Parties") from and against any and all losses, damages, liabilities, obligations, judgments, settlements, costs, and other expenses incurred or suffered by any of Producer's Indemnified expenses incurred or suffered by any Producer's indemnified Parties, whether during or after the term of this Agreement, which is directly or indirectly based upon or related to (i) the breach by Artist of any of her representatives and warranties or a material breach of Artist's covenants and agreements hereunder, or (ii) any acts by Artist relating to Picture or exploitation of Picture.

(c) Procedure. Any party indemnified pursuant to subparagraph (a) or (b) of this Section shall promptly notify the indemnifying party of any claim or litigation from which the indemnification set forth hereunder applies (provided that any failure to promptly notify shall not excuse any indemnification obligations of the indemnitor, except to the extent, if any, to which such failure results in an increase in the liability of the indemnifying party). The indemnifying party shall be obligated to assume, at its sole expense, the defense of any claim or litigation as to which it has indemnification obligation hereunder. If such party fails to so assume its own defense, the indemnifying party shall be obligated to reimburse the indemnified party for any or all expenses (including attorney's fees and expenses) incurred in the defense. If the indemnifying party assumes the defense of the claim, the indemnitee may settle the claims and seek reimbursement from the indemnitor for all costs of the indemnity relating to such settlement.

7. REMEDIES.

(a) Producer's Remedies Cumulative. All remedies accorded herein or otherwise available to Producer and (subject to Section 7 (b) hereof) Artist, shall be cumulative and non-exclusive. No waiver by Producer of any breach of a representation, warranty or covenant shall constitute a waiver of any preceding or subsequent breach of the same representation, warranty or covenant.

(b) Rights Unique. Artist agrees and acknowledges that the rights granted hereunder to Producer are of special, unique, unusual, extraordinary nature, the loss of which may not be responsible or adequately compensated in damages in an action at law, and that Artist's breach of any of their respective obligations hereunder will cause Producer irreparable injury and damage. Accordingly, Artist agrees that in the event of a breach or threatened breach of any of Owner's representations, warranties or covenants hereunder, Producer shall be entitled to appear before any court, agency or body of competent jurisdiction to seek injunctive or equitable relief. To the extent that any such injunctive or equitable relief is granted to Producer, such relief shall not prejudice Producer's right to maintain an action at law to receive money damages.

(c) Artist's Sole Remedies. Artist agrees that in the event of any breach by Producer of any of its representations, warranties or covenants hereunder, Artist's sole remedy in respect in or of such breach shall be an action at law for money and/or damages, if any. In no event shall Artist be entitled to either attempt to rescind this Agreement or to suspend Artist's performance hereunder or seek any equitable or injunctive relief against Producer or its affiliates. Artist agrees not to file or prosecute such equitable or injunctive relief, including, without limitation, any action to enjoin, condition, or restrict production activities of Producer, its affiliates or assigns relating to the Picture or exploitation of the Picture by the Producer, its affiliates, assigns, or any other party.

8. Assignment. Producer shall be entitled to assign any and all of his rights under this Agreement to any party in whole or in part, provided that such assignee assumes in writing

all of Producer's obligations hereunder and provided further that no such assignment shall release Producer of any of its obligations hereunder unless such assignment is to a "major United States Motion Picture Company" as that term is commonly understood, and such company assumes in writing all of the Producer's obligations hereunder, in which case Producer shall have no continuing obligations to Artist following such assignment.

9. Severability. If any of the provisions of this Agreement or the application of any such provisions to the parties hereto with respect to their obligations hereunder, shall be held by tribunal of competent jurisdiction to be unlawful or unenforceable, the remaining provisions of this Agreement shall remain in full force and effect and shall not be affected, impaired or invalidated in any manner.

10. Section Headings. The Section Headings in this Agreement are for convenience of reference only and shall not be used in the construction or interpretation of this Agreement.

11. Notices. All notices or communications hereunder shall be in writing and shall be sent by reputable messenger or telegram to the addresses set forth below or any substitute address previously designated in writing by the addressee. Any such notice shall be deemed to have been received on the day delivered, on any date on which delivery is refused, or the day of transmission by fax or telegram.

If to Artist: (name and address).

If to Producer: (name and address).

12. Application Law. This Agreement shall be governed by and construed in accordance with the laws of the State of California.

13. Entire Agreement. This Agreement constitutes the entire Agreement between the parties hereto pertaining to the subject matter hereof containing all of the covenants and undertakings between the parties with respect to such subject matter. Each representation, inducement, or promise which may have been made and are not embodied herein and in the exhibits hereto, and any and all prior or contemporaneous written and oral agreements between the parties pertaining in any manner to the subject matter of this Agreement expressly are superseded and canceled by this Agreement. This Agreement may not be modified, supplemented or amended except by an instrument signed by the parties to be charged.

Producer:_____ Date:_____

Artist:_____ Date:_____

The Independent Producer
(Your Gateway to Success)

Independent producers are the eyes and ears of the "majors" (major studios). Industry people are watching the independent movement closely. The film industry is always looking for new talent. But they don't want writers without industry credits. The majors watch and wait.

Independent producers still believe in the magic that creates entertaining films. They are not tied down because of big studio politics. They are freer to take chances. Independent producers are hustler, get-the-job-done types. They believe they can make good films, and usually do. They are accessible to the agent-less screenwriter and the screenwriter without industry credits. The independent producer is the newcomers' best chance.

Major studios are virtually inaccessible to beginning writers who don't have agents. Many larger studios will not even read a script unless it is written by a Writers Guild of America (WGA) member. Yet you cannot become a Guild member until you accumulate enough points. So it's a *catch-22* situation. It is the independent producer who may help an agent-less screenwriter gain entry into the film industry.

Independent producers sometimes have difficulty raising the funds they need to produce their projects. For that reason they often turn to foreign financing which frees them from the politics and restraints of the major studios.

Independent producers are not locked into using only A- list writers and talent. This often minimizes the financial risks to individual independent producers, and gives them more freedom to keep a creative thumb on their projects.

Selling a script to an independent producer is the most realistic way for a beginning screenwriter to break into the highly-competitive, feature-film market today.

Independents can take chances which majors cannot. This is one reason that I wanted to write this book—to give beginning screenwriters more options (excuse the pun). Instead of searching for years to find an agent who might be willing to take a chance on a newcomer to get your script into the major market, you can submit directly to independent producers after you query them.

Independent producers cannot afford the high fees and salaries paid by the majors (which can amount to hundreds of thousands of dollars).

Am I impressed by the independent producer? You bet. I have a deep respect for them. They are willing to take a chance on a beginning, unproduced, and agent-less screenwriter. Independent producers are always looking for fresh material. They are the artists of the film industry— the dreamers, the true believers.

Independents look for low-to-medium budget films to produce, so keep this in mind when you are submitting material to them. Don't send them an *Independence Day* sort of script. That's unrealistic. Don't send them action films with lots of demolition derby-type scenes and explosions. These run budgets into the millions. Keep special effects to a minimum.

Meet Independent Film & Television Producers

Marketing a screenplay to the independent film producer requires that you do your homework. Learn the business of screenwriting. Remember that the independents produce low budget films. Don't send a script with bigger-than-life action and a lot of special effects, or an epic that requires hundreds of extras. The independent film has limited scenes and limited locations. Don't write scenes that would need to be shot in exotic places. The independent film is character driven. So know your market.

Selling your screenplay to the independent producer won't get you a six-figure deal. It could, however, get you a sale. The upfront money is negotiable. And you stand a better chance of actually seeing your screenplay produced.

Having two projects in development has opened many doors for me. Credits are very important in the film industry and every credit moves you further along your career path.

Most independent producers have limited office staff; some producers may have only one person helping them out. So don't waste their time. Before you query a producer, ask yourself the following questions:

1) Is your script the best that it can be?

2) Have you written a low budget script?

3) Are you sending a script in the same genre for which the producer is currently looking? (If a producer is looking for a drama, don't send a comedy. You will be wasting his or her time, and yours.)

While updating my Independent Producer List for this book, a producer shared an experience with me that I will now share with you. He said, "We *actually* got a call in the office the other day from a screenwriter who said that he had a great idea, but that he didn't have a fax machine or an email address! So he couldn't submit his pitch in the manner we usually accept. He asked if he could pitch his idea over the phone. I put his call on the speakerphone so my assistant could hear, too. After listening to his pitch, my assistant said, 'Isn't that the same plot as *Independence Day*?' The writer thought about it for a minute and said, 'Oh, yeah. I guess it is.' "

The next time a screenwriter calls that producer he might not be as willing to give another screenwriter a chance, since the previous writer had not thought about his storyline being so similar to a major motion picture. In other words, he hadn't done his homework.

Another independent producer shared more insights with me. He said, "One of the observations I've made over the years about screenwriting is that many people don't think of it in the same terms as they do other disciplines. No one imagines they could wake up one morning and play the saxophone or fly an airplane. But scores of people think that they can fall out of bed and write a screenplay."

Many independent producers I have consulted with have had various concerns about screenwriters sending unsolicited material. To help you out, I am including some of these main concerns here.

Unsolicited Material

Most new writers are unfamiliar with this unwritten law: **Never send your material to a producer without getting permission first.** Sending it without permission is considered sending "unsolicited material." Send a query letter first, along with a self-addressed, stamped envelope.

The phrase, "Shooting yourself in the foot!" applies here. Sending a screenplay without first sending a query letter starts you off on the wrong foot.

Realize the potential inconvenience and legalities in which you may put producers or other industry professionals when you send your screenplay without a query first. Producers must protect themselves. Most new writers are concerned that people want to steal their ideas or work, even though this situation doesn't occur very often. Just cover yourself by registering or copywriting your script *before* you begin pitching it or even sending it out. Most of the stories have been told already. The phrase, "There's nothing new under the sun!" applies here. It's the innovative way in which you tell your version that will make your story unique. Because so many new writers are concerned about theft of their material, producers must protect themselves. They may do so by insisting that new writers first sign release forms. Otherwise, the producers may decide not to read the material at all. You must give them that choice.

There may be various reasons why producers may reject your script. They may not be looking for new material or they may not have the time to read it. On the other hand, if a producer agrees to read your screenplay, he or she will contact you and let you know how to proceed. It's his or her call. Give him/her the opportunity to refuse or accept it.

Never assume that every producer is dying to read your screenplay. Initial contact (*before* sending your script) is imperative.

Following is an example from my own experience. My website address is www.screenwritersutopia.com/pros/callingcard.html. When my email address is listed on the site I receive several pieces of unsolicited material every week. The writers have not asked if they could send their scripts or novels to me by email—they just sent them. Because of my hectic schedule I'm unable to work with new writers except on a limited basis. I want to help new writers, but when they send material to my email address without querying first it can be inconvenient. Having their material come in with no warning is an imposition. Novels can take two hours to download, tying up my computer. Email attachments from strangers may introduce computer viruses which can completely destroy my hard-drive. So I must be extra cautious about these potential problems, and therefore, follow a strict policy: whenever I receive unsolicited material, I don't read it. Never. I just delete it. I, too, must protect myself. As a writer I am more vulnerable to being accused of theft. The funny thing is, I have huge boxes filled with my own ideas for stories I've yet to begin—and the ideas keep coming.

Potential problems may occur when dealing with other screenwriters and their ideas. For example, if I were working on a story and a scene or character in my script was similar to one in an unsolicited script, I could be faced with a lawsuit even though I've never read that script! Therefore, if and when I agree to work with a new writer, I always insist they sign a release form.

When I spoke with a number of industry insiders about this subject, they said they've had similar experiences. They throw unsolicited scripts received in the mail into the trash unopened or return the material unread. They also pass on these writers' names to other industry people, making them aware of their unprofessionalism.

Sending unsolicited material is a true sign of a novice writer—of one who clearly has not taken the time to learn the basic rules for submitting material professionally.

The list of producers in this book is only a sampling of the hundreds of thousands of independent film and television producers worldwide. These producers are everywhere. And you do *not* need an agent to write to them. Just be respectful. They may open doors to your film career.

I have queried each of them and they all gave me permission to list them in this book. Most have their own websites. Review their sites first to learn how they wish to be contacted. To maintain their individual styles, the producers had their own specifications for their listings. Some have listed more information than others. I decided that an informal format is the best way to introduce these talented, creative people to you. Although informal, the list is up-to-date and accurate (at press time). Before contacting anyone, remember:

1) Do your homework; and
2) Always query before sending a script.

If you do not have a computer, get one. Owning a computer is a huge part of your business. It's invaluable as a networking tool. The computer puts you in touch with film industry people worldwide. Buying a computer is an investment in your future and your career. A computer links you to the rest of the world. Having email access reduces your phone bills as well.

When I first started out, my phone bills were thousands of dollars. Now I rarely use the telephone. Sending email is much more convenient and cost effective. Independent producers can answer you when they have the time. If you call when they are busy you may never hear from them again. Almost everyone in the film industry sends emails. Join the 21st century. Many useful websites are listed in this book to help you. New sites are going online daily, so update your own files often.

Every segment of this book offers valuable lessons for marketing your own script without an agent. No one can do the marketing for you. However, by writing this book, I hope to motivate and guide you toward selling your script.

I feel obligated to inform you that while marketing your own script without an agent you should never negotiate your first contract. Contracts can be several pages long or just one or two. This is where you need an entertainment attorney to help you. One well-known entertainment attorney whom I highly recommend has written several books on this subject. His name is Mark Litwak. His practice includes work in the following areas: copyright, trademark, contracts, multimedia law, intellectual property, and book publishing. His website address is: www.marklitwak.com. It provides valuable information and excerpts from his many books.

Independent producers can become your mentors. As a new writer, you should appreciate their experience, artistic vision, and individuality. In my opinion, they provide the best opportunity to make your first sale without an agent.

Again, before initiating contact with any producer, visit his or her website, get to know the company's credits, and find out what type of projects interest the company the most.

Feel free to let me know of your progress and any success you may experience (see my contact information at the back of this book). If you want to share tips with me, I will pass them on to other screenwriters. The film business will prosper if talented screenwriters support each other.

Note:

The author and publishers do not endorse any of the producers listed in this book or guarantee results of any sales of scripts. We suggest that you do the following:

1) Always send a query letter (with a self-addressed, stamped envelope or send an email) *before* you mail out any of your material.

2) Always copyright or register material that you are marketing.

Feedback concerning any of the producers listed in this book is always welcome.

List of Independent Film & TV Producers

A Line Production Company
Willem Symoens
www.alineproduction.com

All She Wrote
Post Office Box 2385
Grass Valley, CA 95945
USA
www.allshewrote.com

Alliance Atlantis Communications, Inc.
Corporate Communications
Phone: 416.966.7710
solang.bernard@allianceatlantis.com

Anabasis
6708 Aldea Avenue
Van Nuys, CA 91406
USA
Phone: 818.881.6025
www.anabasis.com

> They do not accept unsolicited screenplays or manuscripts. They want you to review their website first and read their agreement. If you agree to it, they may request a one-page synopsis for review. Afterwards, they may or may not request a hard copy of your script or manuscript. If an individual calls directly, he or she will be referred to their website or asked to fax a one-page synopsis for review.

Animas Pictures, Inc.
835 Main Avenue, Suite 201
Durango, CO 81301
USA
Phone: 907.385.8686
www.animaspictures.com

> They produce feature films, TV programming, docu-mentaries, "The Earth's Entertainment Nature Video

Series," and children's videos for worldwide theatrical, television, video and Internet markets.

AnvilPix
Kingswood Road
Bethesda, MD 20814
USA
Phone: 301.526.1264

Ashley Productions, LLC
5225 Canyon Crest Drive, #71-340
Riverside, CA 92507-6628
USA
Phone: 909.781.6597, ext. 217
www.ashleyproductions.com

Ashley Productions, A division of 567128 B.C. Ltd.
5870 Lincoln Street
Vancouver, BC V5R 4P7
Canada
www.ashleyproductions.com

Association of Austrian Film Producers (aafp)
Speisingerstrasse 121
A-1130 Vienna
Austria
Phone/Fax: + 43 1 888 96 22
Email: aafp@austrian-film.com
www.austrian-film.com

Avatar Films
121 West 19th Street, Suite 9-D
New York, NY 10011
USA
Phone: 646.486.6873
Fax: 646.486.6875
www.avatarfilms.com

Robin Lim, President
Jason Leaf, Distribution Manager

Bad Kitty Films
2431 Mission Street
San Francisco, CA 94110
USA
Cat Phone: 415.642.MEOW
Fax: 415.723.7378
Email/Queries: query@badkittyfilms.com
www.badkittyfilms.com

Barnstorm Productions
68 Charles Street
Meriden, CT 06450
USA
Phone: 203.237.1462
Fax: 203.639.8000
www.barntv.com

Bastard Amber Productions
1055 Bernard, #6
Outremont, Quebec H2V 1V1
Canada
Email: graveyardalive@hotmail.com

Big Star Entertainment Group, Inc.
Frank A. Deluca, President
13025 Yonge Street, Suite 201
Richmond Hill, Ontario L4E 1A4
Canada

Black Knight Productions, Inc.
1470 Jamaica Road
Marco Island, FL 34145
USA

Blackfish Films
2900 Affirmed CT., Suite D
Lexington, KY 40509
USA
Phone: 859.312.5055
www.blackfishfilms.com

Blackwatch Communications, Inc.
1410 Stanley Street, Suite 606
Montreal, Quebec H3A 1P8
Canada

William R. Mariani, President
Kimberley Berlin, Producer

Blurgirl Productions
Post Office Box 591686
San Francisco, CA 94159-1686
USA
Phone: 415.751.2545
Fax: 415.933.6208
Email: rossana@blurgirl.com
www.blurgirl.com

Creators of film and video in a group effort with
artists, poets, and musicians.

Brimstone Productions
Kevin Lindenmuth
7900 State Street
Brighton, MI 48116
USA
www.lindenmuth.com

Brimstone is a motion picture company specializing
in horror and science fiction films for the home video
market. Founded by Kevin J. Lindenmuth.

Broken Rules Productions
2208 Overland Court
Lexington, KY 40515-1937
USA
Email: brokenrules@brokenrules.net
www.brokenrules.net

BUCK Productions, Inc.
543 Richmond Street, Suite 125
Toronto, Ontario M5V 1Y6
Canada

Phone: 416.362.3330
Fax: 416.362.3336
Email: sbuckley@buckproductions.com
www.buckproductions.com

Contact: Sean Buckley, Owner/Director/Producer

Buffalo Gal Pictures, Inc.
777-70 Arthur Street
Winnipeg, Manitoba R3B 1G7
Canada
Phone: 204.956.2777
Fax: 204.956.7999
Email: bgal@mts.net
www.buffalogalpictures.mb.ca

Bunk Films
Tino Marquez, Jr., President
Post Office Box 47096
Indianapolis, IN 46247
USA
Phone: 317.767.1189
www.bunkfilms.com

C & C TV Productions
321 Kingsly Lane
American Canyon, CA 94503
USA
Toll Free: 800.385.5002
Phone: 707.557.8548
Fax: 707.643.NEWS
www.CNCTV.com

Cambium Entertainment Corp.
18 Dupont Street
Toronto, Ontario M5R 1V2
Canada
Phone: 416.964.8750
Fax: 416.964.1980
Email: cambium@cambiumentertainment.com
www.cambiumentertainment.com

Camera Guys
Post Office Box 40
Forest Knolls, CA 94933
USA
www.camguys.com

> "We make film, video, and Web media adventures:
> 'Camera Guys' by day; independent filmmakers by night."

Camera Guys
Rua dos Mundurucus, 1907
Dept. 1002
Belem 66.000 Para –
Brazil
www.camguys.com

Carnival Films
John Duffy
2546 Kansas Avenue, #102
Santa Monica, CA 90404
USA

> "People should query before sending unsolicited material."

Carpe Diem International Productions
Krista Errickson, COO
Via Cavalier D'Arpino #30
Rome 00197
Italy
Phone: 011 39 06 3600 4542
Cell: 393487903109 (from within Italy: 03487902109)
Uff: 063216015,7

Catdog Films
Email: mail@catdogfilms.co.uk
www.catdogfilms.co.uk

> Catdog made its debut with *AKA Suicide*—an action
> adventure short. Then came *Dead Ended*—a spine chilling
> thriller/horror film set in Oxford at night. *Sixfootunder* is set
> to go into production. Catdog scripts, films, and post produces
> films of all genres: action, horror, thrillers, suspense, etc. They

say, "If you have a script idea, music score, or anything you want to be taken further, send it to us! We are always interested in what other people can produce—whatever their age, career, or experience.

Cellar Door Productions
Gretha Rose, President
3 Malahu Drive
Charlottetown, Prince Edward Island C1A 8A5
Canada
Phone: 902.628.3880
Fax: 902:628.2088
Email: productions@isn.net

City Beach Films, Inc.
12920 Hibiscus Avenue
Seminole, FL 33776
USA
Phone: 727.399.2217
Fax: 727.399.1787
Email: citybeach@aol.com
www.citybeachfilms.com

> City Beach Films is a full service production company based in New York, California, and Florida.

Cityscape Productions
20 Baif Boulevard
Post Office Box 305
Richmond Hill, Ontario L4C 8T1
Canada
Phone: 905.770.0155
> Their "Writer's Department" lists open writers' positions and how to submit material.
> Credit: *The Danny Gayle Show* (TV)

Claddagh Films
Somerset Studios
Aughinish (near Kinvara)
County Clare
Ireland

Phone: + 353 65 7078077
Email: info@claddagh.ie
www.claddagh.ie

Claddagh Films is an independent film and TV production
company based in Galway in the west of Ireland.
Credits: *The Galway Arts Festival, A Place in My Heart,* and
A Talk in the Dark.

Comforty Media Concepts
2145 Pioneer Road
Evanston, IL 60201
USA
Phone: 847.475.0791
Fax: 847.475.0793
Email: comforty@comforty.com
www.comforty.com

"Our Mission is to create programs that reflect the
social issues of our day and our history."

Connections Productions
91 Driscoll Crescent
Moncton, New Brunswick E1E 4C8
Canada
Phone: 506.382.3984
Fax: 506.382.3980

Cool Blue Pictures, Inc.
Post Office Box 82476
Baton Rouge, LA 70884
USA

Specializes in people, humor, and action commercials.

Corcos Media & Entertainment
Post Office Box 5157
Fair Oaks, CA 95628
USA
www.corcus.net

Cornerstone Pictures, Inc.
112 S. Blount Street
Raleigh, NC 27601
USA
www.cornerstonepictures.com

A full-service video and multimedia productions company.

Creanspeak Productions, LLC
223 Flanders Road, #2
Niantic, CT 03635
USA
Phone in CT: 860.739.6286
Phone in LA: 310.801.5562
Fax: 860.739.6287

A full service independent production company that finances under $10 million.

Crimson Pictures
Brian Darling, Executive Producer
www.crimsonpictures.com

Cullen Robertson Productions, Inc.
#408-8623 Granville Street
Vancouver, BC
Canada
V6P 5A1

Cypress Films, Inc.
The Film Center
630 Ninth Avenue, Suite 415
New York, NY 10036
USA
Phone. 212.262.3900
Fax. 212.263.3925
Email: info@cypressfilms.com
www.cypressfilms.com

Cypress Films is a New York based independent film and TV production company with filmography, corporate, information, project details, and more. They say, "We are interested in independent dramas and comedies, with anticipated budgets ranging from $750,000 to $2 million. We are most drawn to edgy or offbeat subjects within a broad range of genres. We accept email or letter submissions of synopses and will request a script if the subject matter is of interest to us."

Deja View® Video Productions
417 S. El Dorado Street
San Mateo, CA 94402
USA
Phone: 650.343.8899
www.djaview.com

Delaney & Friends Cartoon Productions
105 West 3rd Avenue
Vancouver, BC V5Y 1E6
Canada
Phone: 604.877.8585
Fax: 604.877.1614
www.delaneyandfriends.com

"We are an independent animation production company specializing in 2-D animation for film and television. Unless financing is attached we do not normally accept unsolicited scripts."

Dependent Films
Peter James Zielinski, President
Timothy Soszko, Vice President
12042 Elm Drive
Blue Island, IL 60406
USA
Phone: 309.454.3255
Contact: pjz@dependentfilms.net
www.dependentfilms.net

Devine Entertainment Corporation
Maral Bablanian, General Manager
2 Berkeley Street, Suite 504
Toronto, Ontario M5A 2W3
Canada
Phone: 416.364.2282
Fax: 416.364.1440
Email: devinent@interlog.com
www.devine-ent.com
Interactive: www.devinetime.com

Diane Films
Contact: Francesca Prada
Email: Dianefilms@AOL.com

> Offices in San Francisco, New York, and Los Angeles. Their
> submission policy: send a query letter with a synopsis and
> credits/credentials. Unsolicited manuscripts returned
> unread. No electronic attachments. Genres: art and genre
> films. Budget range: open. Preference: strong literary value,
> solid dramatic structure, good character development,
> interesting dialogue, compelling plots.

DIKENGA Multimedia
Steve Balderson
Post Office Box 368
Wamego, KS 66547
USA
Fax: 785.458.6000
www.dikenga.com

DNA Development
223 W. Lancaster Avenue
Devon, PA 19333
USA
Phone: 800.576.2001
www.mecfilms.com/dna

DoubleDown Films
Chicago, IL
USA
www.info@doubledownfilms.com

Dream Productions
43 Abdel Reheem Sabry Street, Agousa
Ground floor – Flat 2
Cairo
Egypt
Phone/Fax: 202.3359524
Mobile: 2012.3117598 (Ahmed Rashwan – GM)
Email: dreamprod_egypt@yahoo.com

Drop Dead Films
41 Watchung Plaza, Suite 185
Montclair, NJ 07042
USA
www.dropdeadfilms.com

> "Although we do not accept unsolicited material (since
> we mainly develop in house), we frequently answer
> questions and offer advice to any aspiring artists."

Earthrealm Entertainment
2028-D Brentwood Road
Raleigh, NC 27604
USA
Phone: 919.876.6927
Email: info@earthrealm.com
www.earthrealm.com

> Contact: Stephen C. Seward
> Email: brainstorm@earthrealm.com
> Earthrealm is an independent film company based in
> Raleigh, NC. Home of *Blooderfly – The Wrath of Gaia*.

Echo Film Productions, Inc.
407 W. Bannock
Boise, ID 83702
USA
www.echofilms.com

Edgewood Studios

Attention: David Giancola
Howe Center Unit 12B, Suite 90
Rutland, VT 05701
USA
Phone: 802.773.0510
Fax: 802.773.3481
www.edgewoodstudios.com

"We only accept submissions via the mail. NO email submissions. Thank you."

ei Independent Cinema

68 Forest Street
Montclair, NJ 07042
USA
Phone: 973.509.1616
Fax: 973.509.3530
Email: eiCinema@aol.com
www.eiCinema.com

Eightball Films

167 N. Racine
Chicago, Illinois 60607
USA
Phone: 312.492.6669
www.eightballfilms.com

Embryo Films

Sydney
Australia
www.embryo-films.com

A Sydney-based feature film production company, seeking Australian or New Zealand content. Offers screenwriting workshop/development programs in Australia and New Zealand. They produce documentaries, dramas, commercials, and corporate films. They're currently building a series of screenwriting workshops into a full-fledged development program for independent films. Because they originally received so many scripts that were simply awful, they're now building a whole development program for new and intermediate writers. (Advanced writers have even expressed an interest in it). They're expecting to see this expand during the next year.

Emerald Oceans Entertainment
An EOMedia Group Company
Ryan B. Smith, President
Quinn Katz, VP Development & Productions
Email: quinn@eomedia.com
Post Office Box 441234
Aurora, CO 80014-1234
USA

Endless Sky Productions
Scott McLain
Box 130332
St. Paul, MN 55113
USA
Pager: 612.228.4682

> "Here at Endless Sky Productions, we feel led to create passionate and heartfelt music and films that will touch lives in a meaningful way."

EnFocus Filmworks, Inc.
3709 S. George Mason Drive
Suite 211-E
Falls Church, VA 22041
USA

Equinox Pictures LLC
6828 Oakland Avenue
Edina, MN 55435
USA

Equinox Pictures LLC
Bispegata 4
2315 Hamar
Norway

An alliance of independent filmmakers—production of narrative, feature length films.

Even Tide Productions
Gary Irwin
www.eventideproductions.com

4 Reel Entertainment
6423 S. Eggleston, 1b
Chicago, IL 60621
USA

The Factory: A & E Productions
Derek Lebrero, CEO- President
2055 Peel Street, Suite 825
Montreal, Quebec H3A 1V4
Canada
Phone: 514.848.9198
Fax: 514:845.5311
Email: factoryfilm@hotmail.com

Fat Lion Pictures, Inc.
Contact: Bill Johnson
44 West 45th Street
New York, NY 10036
USA
Phone: 212.903.4460
www.fatlionpictures.com

A full-service film and video production company offering quality and reliability. They create videos for corporate image, marketing, training, promotional, industrial, medical, entertainment documentaries and commercials, from concept through post-production.

Favourite Vision Ltd.
Office: 18 Hr. Smirnenski Blvd., Sofia 1421
Mail: Post Office Box 66, Sofia 1220
Bulgaria
Phone: (359 2) 659146
Fax: (359 2) 650598
Mobile Phone: +359 88 557151

Email: menev@favouritevision.com
www.favouritevision.com

Fender Bender Films
11920 Chandler Blvd., #116
Valley Village, CA 91302
USA
Fax: 818.623.8632
Email: FenderBenderFilms@aol.com

Sean Kinney and Ross Marti (writers/directors/producers)
Credits: *Rubbernecking* feature film.

Fernbacher Productions
The e-production company
300 Broadway, Suite #37
San Francisco, CA 94133
USA
Phone: 415.434.3376 (e-office)
Phone: 415.264.4964 (e-cell)
Fax: 603.649.0776
Phone: 925.254.2994 (home)
Email: john@fernbacher.com
www.fernbacher.com

FilmDogz
424 South 23rd Street
Wilmington, NC 28403
USA
Phone: 910.254.9219

FilmFilm, Inc.
33 Riverside Drive
New York, NY 10023
USA
www.filmfilm.com

Produces /promotes independent films online.

FilmKitchen.com/Rogue Arts
Post Office Box 40
Hermosa Beach, CA 90254
USA

www.filmkitchen.com

An independent film production and distribution company. Their feature credits include the theatrically-released *Loser, My Sweet Killer,* and *Angel's Ladies.* They are completing *Hard Luck.* Company principles are Kirk Harris (actor/filmmaker), Tom Pellegrini, and Jack Rubio.

Filmline International
410 St-Nicolas Street, Suite 10
Montreal, Quebec H2Y 2P5
Canada

Flying Rhino Productions, Inc.
500 Tamal Plaza, Suite 520
Corte Madera, CA 94925
USA
Voice: 415.927.4466
Fax: 415.927.1197
www.flying-rhino.com

Freelance Productions Limited
1857 Fieldcrest Drive
Sparks, NV 89434
USA
Phone: 775.626.0267

Freelance the Company
Hamed Mahmoud, Director/Producer
www.mandy.com/home.cfm?c=fre045

Hamed Mahmoud has ten years of extensive experience in film production. He is a freelance director and a facilitator of film and video production services in Egypt.

Freestyle Film Production
Producers: Richard Reay & Tom Saunders
9 Ebor Street
Heaton, Newcastle-Upon-Tyne NE6 5DL
United Kingdom
Email: prod@freestyleproductions.freeserve.co.uk
www.freestyleproductions.freeserve.co.uk

Frye Productions
Erica Ferencik, Director of Development
4 Longfellow Place, Suite 3806
Boston, MA 02114
USA
Phone: 617.573.0000
Email: ebgf@aol.com

Services: Screenplay development, film production.

Girlie Girl Productions
1520 North Vista Street, Suite 203
Los Angeles, CA 90046
USA
Phone: 323.851.1206
Fax: 323.851.1263
Email: info@girliegirlproductions.com
www.girliegirlproductions.com

With associates and partnerships on both coasts, they tap
into two creative markets for new material: the Chicago
theatre and film communities. Don't send unsolicited
scripts. Send a short query first—by letter, email or fax. If
they're interested, they'll contact you for further info.

Give A Damn Films
435 Hudson Street, 8th Floor
New York, NY 10014
USA
Phone: 212.633.8389
www.giveadamnfilms.com

Brings writers, directors, and editors together to produce
films for the non-profit community.

Gizmo Filmworks
www.geocities.com/~skylinemovies/

They prefer that you go to their website and follow
directions for submissions.

Gorica Productions
295 Silverbirch Avenue
Toronto, Ontario M4E 3L6
Canada

"Interested in scripts by Canadian authors or scripts with Canadian angle."

Greenhill Productions
216 East 45th Street, 14th Floor
New York, NY 10017
USA

Gulliver Media Australia Pty. Ltd.
Gulliver Film Productions
ABN: 86.010.372.531
Post Office Box 371
Paddington, Brisbane, Qld.
Australia, 4064
Email: info@gullivermedia.com.au
Phone: +617.3367.0899
Fax: +617.3368.2164
Mobile: 0419.657.699 (Larry Zetlin)

Member of Screen Producers Association of Australia

Hellspawn Productions
Ian Grant
Boston, MA
USA
www.horrorflic.com

Specializes in low budge comedy horror films.

Heroic Film Company, Inc.
324 Markham Street
Toronto, Ontario M6G 2K9
Canada

"13 x 30 minutes comedy series *Our Hero* currently airing on CBC."

Hocus Focus Films
Mickey Kovler – General Manager
4 HabeeOr Street
Post Office Box 53323
Tel-Aviv 61533
Israel
Phone: 972.0.3.6470405
Fax: 972.0.3.6483179
Mobile: 972.0.54.294964
Email: kovler@focusfilms.com
www.focusfilms.com

Hollywood East Productions
Post Office Box 2623
Meriden, CT 06450
USA
Phone: 203.235.4286
www.hollywoodeastproductions.com

Hotbed Media
Unsu Lee, Co-President
555 Florida Street, #317
San Francisco, CA 94110
USA
www.hotbed.com

Hudson Productions
380 S.W. Canyon Road
Madras, OR 97741
USA
Email: hudson@hudsonpro.com
www.hudsonpro.com

> They are in production with *The Unknown*, have scheduled
> their next project, but are interested in seeing scripts.

Imagio Productions
Av.N.S.de Copacabana, 583-308
Copacabana – Rio de Janeiro
Brazil
Email: email@imagio.com.br
www.imagio.com.br

Rachel Balassiano, Scriptwriter
Sonia Dias, Executive Producer
Ciro Duarte, Director

Independent Documentary Group/IDG Films
394 Elizabeth Street
San Francisco, CA 94114
USA
Phone: 415.824.5822
Fax: 415.824.0406
Email: idgfilms@earthlink.net
www.idgfilms.com

Christopher Beaver and Judy Irving, Executive Directors
"We primarily produce documentaries, although we've taken the occasional foray into fiction films."

InnerCity Films
Stuart Cianos – General Manager
Post Office Box 305
Redwood City, CA 94064-0305
USA
Email: scianos@innercityfilms.com
www.innercityfilms.com

Main area of focus: Documentary Productions

Innerworld Pictures
5161 #1 Revere Street
Chino, CA 91710
USA
Email: tylertharpe@yahoo.com
www.iwpictures.com

Insanity Filmworks, Inc.
Post Office Box 21030
Mesa, AZ 85277-1030
USA
Fax: 480.325.1495
www.insanityfilms.com

Contact: Jason Francois, Producer, Jason@insanityfilms.com

Insight Film & Video Productions
#103-1675 Hornby Street
Vancouver, British Columbia V6Z 2M3
Canada
Phone: 604.623.3369
Fax: 604.623.3448
Email: insight@insightfilm.com

International Production Company
209 North Doheny Drive
Beverly Hills, CA 90211
USA
Phone: 310.276.6519
Fax: 310.276.6536
Email: ipcfilms@aol.com
www.ipcfilms.com

> From their website: "International Production Co. was
> founded by Tulane University Graduates with a business
> background. Looking for ideas, projects, scripts, and talent."

IVM Productions, Inc.
1801 Collins Avenue, Suite 442
Miami Beach, FL 33139
USA
www.ivmproductions.com

Jaguar Films
Wayne A. Hazle
1317 N. San Fernando Boulevard, #326
Burbank, CA 91504-4272
USA
Phone: 818.247.9250
Fax: 818.247.0241
www.jaguarfilms.com

> Produces challenging films that highlight multicultural
> themes.

JWS Productions, Inc.
8959 S. Elizabeth Street
Chicago, IL 60620
USA
Phone: 773.429.6917
www.jwsproductions.net

KSK Films
12 West 27th Street, 8th Floor
New York, NY 10001
USA
Phone: 212.481.3111 OR: 1.888.KSKFILM
Email: cindy@kskfilms.com
www.kskfilms.com OR www.kskdesign.com

> Manny Kivowitz, Executive Producer/Owner
> Cindy Grey, Supervising Producer/Director of Development

LCA Productions
Paseo Colon del Banco de Costa Rica
125 metros sur casa #222
San Jose
Costa Rica
Post Office Box in Costa Rica: 461-1250 Costa Rica
Post Office Box in USA: SJO 1465
Post Office Box 025216, Miami, Florida 33102-5216
Phone: 506.256.4303
Mobile: 506.384.6417
Fax: 506.256.4306
Email: tv@1caproductions.com

> Film and video production company. TV commercials.
> 35mm and 16mm. Documentaries in Digital Betacam.
> Their main area is commercials but they have also made
> some documentaries.
> Jose Iqnacio Paris, Director/Director of Photography

Leontine Pictures LLC
Pete Menzies: Producer
Post Office Box 221
Bedford Hills, NY 10507
USA

Phone: 914.572.2192
Fax: 914.234.3939
Email: info@leontinepics.com
www.leontinepics.com

Lifeline Entertainment
www.lifelineentertainment.net

Living Spirit Pictures Limited
Ealing Film Group
Ealing Green, London, W5 5EP
United Kingdom
Phone: 020.87588544; Mobile: 07977.516.628
Fax: 020.87588559
Email: mail@livingspirit.com
www.livingspirit.com

M3 Films LLC
96 Morton Street, 4th Floor
New York, NY 10014
USA
Phone: 212.929.8344
www.m3films.com

> Contact: Salvatore Oppedisano, Exec. Producer/Partner
> Production, promotion, and design services for film, TV,
> and animation.

MacMillian Films
10 Belsize Street
Kenmore, 4069 Brisbane QLD.
Australia
Phone: 07.33788172
Mobile: 04111 889811

> Dedicated to projects with a cultural or historical slant.

Mainframe Entertainment, Inc.
Giuliana Bertuzzi, CMA
500-2025 West Broadway
Vancouver, British Columbia V6J 1Z6
Phone: 604.714.2600

Fax: 604.714.2641
Cell: 604.202.6244

Majestic Productions Ltd.
40 House Lane
Arlesey
Beds SG15 6XU
United Kingdom
Phone: 01462.734391 or 07970.028791
Email: majesticstudio@aol.com
www.majesticproductions.co.uk

Makalani Productions and Media Services
Amour Arenzana (Executive Producer/Director)
2311 Hastings Shore Lane
Redwood Shores, CA 94065
USA
Phone: 650.591.7739
Email: amour@makalani.com

Manhattan Filmworks
Harris Solomon
370 Central Park Avenue
Scarsdale, NY 10583
USA
Phone: 914.723.333
Fax: 630.566.7617

> "Manhattan Filmworks projects are totally people-driven.
> The stories told through our film productions are centered
> on individuals. Harris Salomon and Gustavo Letelier believe
> a good film begins not with special effects, but with a unique
> story about people. It's an old-fashioned idea, with a new
> generation outlook."

(Author's Note: The previous description ultimately captures
the creative genius that is the independent producer—the heart
of your vision.)

Mark Archer Entertainment

Attn: Project Submissions
1910 St. Joe Ctr. Road, Suite 22
Fort Wayne, IN 46825
USA
www.TheLifeBetween.com

> They produce films and television series.
> Now in production: *Willy T. Ribbs*, *Paul Newman*, *Mario Andretti*, and *Dan Gurney: The Life Between*.

Marvin Friedman Productions

283 Henry Street
Brooklyn Heights, NY 11201
USA
Phone: 718.858.5373
Email: mf283@aol.com

Media Concepts Group

Kristell Mazzuco, Marketing VP
1712 Don Avenue, Suite B
San Jose, CA 95124
USA
Phone: 408.316.1275
Fax: 650.745.0989
Email: kristell@mconcepts.com
www.mconcepts.com

> A film, video, multimedia design, and production company specializing in the development and use of digital media. Also offers equipment rentals.

Media House Films

Michael Savino/Mark Veau at the Victorian
4 West Broadway
Gardner, MA 01440
USA
Phone: 978.630.3369
Email: markveau@excite.com
Email: msavino@ultranet.com

Media Oblongata Productions
Jeff Pogue
699 Gresham Avenue
Atlanta, GA 30316
USA
Phone: 404.371.0320

Michael Wiese Productions
11288 Ventura Boulevard, Suite 821
Studio City, CA 91604
USA
Phone: 818.379.8799
Fax: 818.986.3408
www.mwp.com

> They make films, publish books about filmmaking, and provide consulting services.

Michael Wiese
2 St. Loy Cottage
St. Loy, St. Buryan
Penzance TR19 6DH England
Phone and Fax: +44 (0) 1736 810 001

Midget Media
Post Office Box 761
Tewksbury, MA 01876
USA
Phone: 978.858.3740
Fax: 978.858.0928
Email: ghouls@midgetmedia.com
www.midgetmedia.com

Midnight Sun Productions
2512 E. Thomas Road, Suite 7
Phoenix, AZ 85016
USA
www.mandy.com/home.cfm?c=mid018

> A multi-award winning, full service video production company. They offer creative to post, and specialize in corporate documentary, training, and entertainment.

Mini Productions
www.miniproductions.com

Mortimer Jones Expeditions
A Film and Video Company
2220 McClintock Road
Charlotte, NC 28205
USA
Phone: 704.373.9005
Email: adamparoo@mortimerjones.com
Email: mortimer@mortimerjones.com

> Adam Paroo and Adam Stone, Producers
> Credits: Valvoline "It Shows" (3 commercials),
> Charlotte Hornets "Superfan Series" (5 commercials series)
> Questa.com "Meet Questro" (3 comm. series for their launch)

Moushel Productions
66 Park Street
Andover, MA 01810
USA

Newborn Pictures
222 St. John Street, Suite 4G
Portland, ME 04102
USA
Phone: 207.761.0110
Fax: 207.771.5320
www.newbornpix.com

> Producers of *Pennyweight* and *Reindeer Games* with trailers
> and a link to "Live on 2 with Kyle and Efram" on cable TV.

Next Wave Films
Santa Monica, CA
USA
www.nextwavefilms.com/fullstory.html

> "This company, of The Independent Film Channel, was
> established to help exceptionally talented filmmakers from
> the United States and abroad to launch their careers. Low
> budget production is the only way for most new filmmakers

to demonstrate their talent, and Next Wave Film seeks to maximize opportunities for these filmmakers."

Nightmare Productions
3905 25th Avenue South
Mpls., MN 55406
USA
Phone: 612.276.1303 or 612.991.1739

Oneira Pictures International
www.aliendog.net

Pelon Films Ltd.
Post Office Box 1369
Even-Yehuda, 40500, Israel
Phone: 972.3.5274317
Fax: 972.3.5274318
Mobil: 972.53.866566 (Eitan)
Mobil: 972.53.866567 (Avner)
www.pelonfilm.com

Peter Rowe Productions, Inc.
Pyman Studios
2196 Dunwin Drive
Mississauga, L5L-1C7
Ontario, Canada

Pop Films
Attn: Dave Laky
707 Park Lake Lane
Norcross, GA 30092
USA
www.popfilms.org
A group of Atlanta filmmakers dedicated to making passionate films.

Poya Pictures, LLC
3100 Riverside Drive, Suite 341
Los Angeles, CA 90027
USA

Phone: 323.309.7692
Fax: 323.661.6057
www.poyapictures.com

Adrian Fulle, Managing Partner
Rick S. Fulle, Executive Producer
David Miller, Producer/General Partner

Prodigy Entertainment
Post Office Box 4899
Mountain View, CA 94040
USA
www.sleepingwiththelion.com

Proteus
c/o Rob Heydon
97 Hamilton Street
Toronto Ontario
Canada M4M 2C7
Phone: 416.406.3777
Fax: 416.499.6963
Email: robheydon@hotmail.com

⚹ Python/Aquarius Productions
Attn: Andrew
388 Broadway
Studio 4 / 2nd Floor
New York, NY 10013
USA
Phone: 212.941.6095
Email: pythonaquarius@yahoo.com
www.pythonaquarius.com

From their website: "Our operations are based in the loft
community of Tribeca, New York City. Our specialty is
independent production with big league potential. Our
vision is unique—we believe in being resourceful by using
a little to make a lot. Our approach is unconventional—
we believe in getting to know our clients and collaborators
on a personal basis. Our success is unparalled. Our
optimism and commitment have helped us to produce
award-winning productions time and again."

Qwato International Studio ®
Email: contact@qwato.com
www.qwato.com

A film and interactive entertainment studio.
Contact: Scott Frost.

RCW MediaWorks
Post Office Box 55463
Phoenix, AZ 85078-5463
USA
Email: rcw@rcwmediaworks.com
www.rcwmediaworks.com

"Showcasing our films including critics corner, casting
call, trailers, and short stories."

Real World Productions
2217 2nd Avenue North, Suite 306
Birmingham, AL 35203
USA
Phone: 205.715.0003
Email: realworld@mindspring.com
www.realworldproductions.org

"Small but full service (productions, post, music mixing,
animation, film camera) production company."

Realitory Productions
4724 Conejo Avenue
Woodland Hills, CA 91364
USA
Phone: 818.404.8711
Fax: 818.702.8611
www.Realitory.com

Monica Ramone, Producer/Partner (Monica@Reality.com)
Michael Condro, Writer/Director/VFX (MAC@Reality.com)
Television shows, films, commercials, music videos,
corporate videos, Web content, digital (G-4), editing, VFX."

Red Card Films

Attn: Kevin Hines
197 East Fifth Avenue
Berea, OH 44017
USA

RedHouse Films

Post Office Box 111751
Campbell, CA 95011-1751
USA
Phone: 408.378.FILM (3456)
Email: contact@redhousefilms.com
www.redhousefilms.com

> San Francisco Bay Area's first independent motion picture company and studio. Founded by Adam Ray. Indie writers, directors, actors, cinematographers, editors, and effects.

Road Dog Productions

David Lowery
Email: ghost-boy@juno.com
www.road-dog-productions.com

> Road Dog Productions is an independent production company run by David Lowery, the writer/director of the feature film *Lullaby*. They do not option scripts or treatments, but will assist filmmakers in getting their own projects off the ground. Official site of the producers of *The Riff* and other independent films.

SaGA Film & Video Production

71000 Sarajevo
Hakije Kulenovica 7
Bosnia and Herzegovina
Phone/Fax: 387.33.666.811, 471 145
Email: saga@sagafilm.com
www.sagafilm.com

> Ismet Nuno Arnautalic, Producer
> "SaGA Film Production Company is a film production company in Bosnia and Herzegovina that produced documentary films and two feature films during the war."

Salmac Productions
Sally McLean, Creative Director
Email: films@salmac.com
www.salmac.com

"It is actually our policy to only accept unsolicited material from screenwriters (and crew) via email, as it makes it easier for us to target those projects (and people) we are interested in. We are heavily committed at the moment with our current films, but anything can change at a moment's notice in this industry, especially in the independent sector. Please send a logline or brief synopsis to our email address along with your contact details."

Saltshaker Productions
Felicia Middlebrooks, President/CEO
200 East Chestnut Street, Suite 1021
Chicago, IL 60611
USA
Phone: 312.867.1424

San Juan Productions
Scott Ransom, DP
Box 1100
Telluride, CO 81435
USA
Phone: 970.728.4257
Santori Productions
Post Office Box 1262
Grass Valley, CA
USA
www.allshewrote.com

SFINX FILM/TV ApS
Solvgade 92A Baghuset
1307 Copenhagen K
Denmark
Phone: +45.33323253
Fax: +45.33914490
Email: info@sfinx-film.dk
www.sfinx-film.dk

"An independent production company of mainly serious quality documentaries, presently working with themes treating migration and cultural diversity. We are also engaged in developing a multicultural youth-program for Danish TV. Many of our films have won national and independent awards, and have been broadcast as widely as DRTV, TV2/Denmark, Finnish YLEI & Yle2, Swedish SVT, French La Sept Arte, Hungary, Poland, Australia, Japan and Saudi Arabia. We have also worked with fiction and are developing several projects."

Credits: *Birds in a Cage, War is Not for Children, Ditching Dummies, Two Women on a River, They Don't Burn Priests, Do They?*

SHADE
1615 Mellwood Avenue
Louisville, KY 40206
USA
Phone: 502.589.0827
Fax: 502.589.5023
www.shadeent.com

"We are fortunately one of the few, full service 'truly independent' feature film companies in Kentucky."

Shoehorn Productions
Visnja R. Clayton
Email: info@shoehornproductions.com
www.shoehornproductions.com

Film, New Media, and Web development services:
Film: Producing, directing, costume design, script supervising, digital video production.
New Media: CD Rom development, video editing, streaming media services, Flash.
Web Development: Technical consulting, knowledge management consulting, Web application and Website development.

Siete Machos Films
216 East 45th Street, 14th Floor
New York, NY 10017
USA

Silicon Daydream Productions, Ltd.
Attn: Graham B. Wilson
6700 Franklin Place, #403
Hollywood, CA 90028
USA
Phone: 323.463.4905
Mobile: 323.314.0449
Email: info@sdp3d.com

Silicon Daydream Productions, Ltd.
Corporate Office:
3454 S. Columbine Circle
Englewood, CO 80110
USA
Phone: 303.761.4442
www.info@sdp3d.com/contact.htm

Sirk Productions, LLC
2460 Lemoine Avenue, 3rd Floor
Fort Lee, NJ 07024
USA
Phone: 201.944.0982
Email: sirkprod@yahoo.com
www.sirkproductions.com

An independent film and television company.

Skyline Productions, Inc.
2111 East Baseline Road, Suite A-1
Tempe, AZ 85283
USA
Toll Free: 1.877.211.7486
Phone: 408.345.8009
Fax: 408.345.8101
Email: joe@skylinevideo.com
www.skylinevideo.com

Joe Reynolds, Owner

Soapbox Productions, Inc.
312 Stevens Drive
West Vancouver, British Columbia
V7S 1C6
Phone: 604.983.2555
Fax: 604.983.2558
Email: soapboxproductions@telus.net

Sound Venture International, Inc.
Neil Bregman
219-126 York Street
Ottawa, Ontario
Canada K1N 5T5
Phone: 613.241.5111
Fax: 613.241.5010
Cell: 613.769.5828
www.soundventure.com

Space Viz Productions
Phone/Fax: 646.356.0041
www.spaceviz.com

> Contact: Mark Moidel, Director/Producer/writer/narrator/ Senior Designer. Mostly documentary productions, featuring Sir Arthur C. Clarke and Buzz Aldrin. Other productions will be considered.

Steel Cow Productions
204 W. 87th Street, #45
New York, NY 10024
USA
Email: steelcowfilms@yahoo.com
www.steelcow.com

> Producers of *Fat Chance: The Movie.*

Sterling Pacific Films/Loch Lomond Entertainment Ltd.
Feature Film and Television
228 Main Street, Suite One
Venice, CA 90291
USA

> Independent film and television development company.

Sterling Pictures
53 Great Portland Street
London W1W 7LG
United Kingdom
www.sterlingpictures.com

> Independent film and television production company.
> Producer: Michael Riley

Studionext
427 Broadway
New York, NY 10013
USA
Phone: 212.334.6398
Fax: 212.343.8269
www.studionext.com

> M. Gabriel Brodherson, Assistant Head of Production/
> Original Programming

Steven Weill Productions, Inc.
250 West 26th Street
New York, NY 10001
USA
Phone: 212.367.9599
www.stevenweill.com

Suggs Media Productions, Inc.
156 West 44th Street, 7th Floor
New York, NY 10036
USA

Telescene Film Group, Inc.
5705 rue Ferrier
Montreal, Quebec
H4P 1N2
Canada
Phone: 514.737.5512
Fax: 514.737.7945
Email: information@telescene.com

The May Street Group Film, Video & Animation, LTD.
1274 May Street
Victoria, British Columbia V8V 2T2
Canada
Phone: 250.380.6656
Fax: 250.380.6670
Email: maystreet@pinc.com

TOOLS Productions
65 N. Moore Street
New York, NY 10013
USA
www.thetools.com

Toronto Pictures
www.torontopictures.com

> "We do not accept scripts. We do not accept unsolicited
> material. We only consider new project proposals. If a
> writer wants to propose a project, he/she must follow the
> process outlined on our website in 'CAREERS'. The
> applicant should provide us with his/her name, city, and
> country of residence, phone number, and email address.
> He/she has to let us know what kind of project he/she is
> proposing, the budget and the available funds."

Tri Media Production Services Limited
5112 Prince Street, 2nd Floor West
Halifax, Nova Scotia B3J 1L3
Canada
Phone: 902.422.8816
Fax: 902.422.1580

Contact: F. Whitman Trecartin, President

TVA International
Maite Martinez Communications
Phone: 514.284.2525, #2025
Fax: 514.985.4460
Email: mmartinez@tva-international.com

TYPE Pre-productions and Talent Company and News Coverage

Paseo Colon del Banco de Cost Rica 125 metros sur. casa #222
Post Office Box in Costa Rica: 461-1250
San Jose
Costa Rica
Address in USA:
SJO 1465 Post Office Box 25216
Miami, Florida 33102-5216
USA
Phone: 506.256.4303
Mobile: 506.384.6417
Fax: 506.256.4306
Email: jparis@sol.racsa.co.cr

Jose Ignacio Paris, President/Partner
Pre-production and talent company. They also have Film News production for *Inside Edition* (Kingworld).

Underdog Entertainment

Post Office Box 98765
Sandton
Johannesburg 2146
South Africa
Phone: +27 11 380 3232
Fax: +27 11 380 3233
Email: info@underdog.co.za
Email: isabel@underdog.co.za

Marc Schwinges, Executive Producer
Luiz DeBarros, Director
Isabel van Niekerk, Marketing Director
"A new generation, cutting-edge entertainment company that understands both digital and traditional media. We make use of the finest award-winning film and television directors, writers, Web designers, and multimedia gurus to redefine the connections of media entertainment both in form and content."

Urban Outlaw Productions
Astoria, NY
USA
www.urbanoutlaw.com

Verseau International, Inc.
225 Roy Street, East
Montreal, Quebec
H2W 1M5
Canada
Phone: 524.848.9814
Fax: 524.848.9908
Email: courrier@verseauintl.com

Producers: Aimee Danis and Daniele Bussy

Waverly Motion Pictures, LLC
4104 Woodbridge Road
Peabody, MA 01960
USA
Phone: 978.535.8678
Email: waverlyMPS@aol.com
Bill Aydelott, President
My original claim to fame in independent productions was
as producer and cameraman for John Sayles' first feature,
The Return of the Secaucus Seven.

Welter Productions
7931 Kessler Street
Overland Park, KS 66204
USA
Email: newbiz@danwelter.com

White Pine Pictures
862 Richmond Street West
Suite 201
Toronto, Ontario M6J 1C9
Canada

Wild Rose Films
Post Office Box 572
Beverly Hills, CA 90213-0572

USA
Email: wildrosefilms@wldrse.com

Yankee Classic Pictures
1751 Beacon Street, Suite 300
Brookline, MA 02445
USA
Phone: 617.975.0285
Email: info@yankeeclassic.com

President: J.P. Ouellette
Submission requests to: Lauren Evers

Your Half Pictures, LLC
1639 11th Street, Suite 110
Santa Monica, CA 90404
USA
Phone: 310.664.1088
Fax: 310.664.3743
Email: josh@yourhalf.com OR ryan@yourhalf.com
www.yourhalf.com
Producers: Josh R. Jaggars, Ryan Harper, and Rusty Gray

Zephyr Productions
516 Gretchen Court
Greensboro, NC 27410
USA
Phone: 336.855.1960
Fax: 336.855.1960 (call first before faxing/manual set)
Email: zephyr16@hotmail.com

Barbara Rosson Davis, Producer/Writer
Motion pictures, television, animation, "Zit" flicks (Internet
short films), film content, spec scripts.
Credits: *Echoes, Inside the World of Jesse Allen (Vorpal),
The Awakener, Sacred Fire, The Velvet Hour, Word of Mouth,
What's in a Name?, The FRUITeeNIES, Martin Martinis
and the Golden Toothpick of James Cagney.*

Zokalo Entertainment
www.zokalo.com

Writers can email a one-page synopsis to the Head of Development, Chris Sablan (chris@zokalo.com), or check the website for submission details. They specialize in producing character driven films, with a strong appeal to the international market.

FLASH: "As we get closer to finishing the post production of our film, *No Turning Back*, and prepare to hit the film festival circuit, we are proud to announce the launching of our new website: www.noturningback.com".

Zone 5 Pictures

www.zone5pictures.com

There is a lot of information on their website, so check it out for yourself.

Film Commissions

Use the following resource list to become familiar with film activities in your local community. There are film commissions all over the world and they can also help you find independent film producers in your area.

Film commissions promote film and television production and assist in the development of the local film industry. Some provide expert advice on area talent, facilities, locations, script development, fellowships, production investments, and new media activities.

Read these and other individual websites (or write to the email addresses) to find filming news and publications in your area. In most cases they are a valuable resource for local film activities.

Alabama Film Office
www.telefilm-south.com/Alabama.Alabama.html

Amador County Film Commission
www.volcano.net/~filmamador/

> The Amador County Film Commission is the acting liaison between film companies and the County of Amador, City of Amador, City of Ione, City of Jackson, City of Plymouth, and the City of Sutter Creek in CA.

Arctic Circle:

1. Barents Euro Arctic Region
   Barents Euro Arctic Film Commission
   www.beafc.com
2. Norwegian Film Commission – Bergen
   www.norwegian-filmcom.org
3. Film on Gotland
   www.filmpagotland.org/gfc
4. West Swedish Screen Commission
   www.wssc.org

Austria:

1. Austrian Film Commission (AFC) Website: www.afc.at/
2. Location Austria Website: www.location-austria.at
3. Triol – Cine Tirol Website: www.cine

Australian Film Commission
www.afc.gov.au

British Columbia Films
www.bcfilm.bc.ca

British Film Commission
www.britfilmcom.co.uk

California Film Commission
www.commerce.ca.gov/business/select/film

Canada Film and TV Productions Association, The
www.cftpa.ca/main.html

Central Virgina Film Office
www.cvfo.org/hall/fvares.htm

Chicago Film Office
www.cityofchicago.org/specialeffects/filmoffice

Colorado Film Office
www.coloradofilm.org

East Midlands Screen Commission
www.emsc.org.uk

El Paso Film Commission
www.elpasocvb.com/film

Film Florida
www.floridafilm.com/index.cfm

France

1. Commission National du Film France
   www.filmfrance.com

2. Aquitaine Region – Aquitaine Tournages
   (Fax: 33.5.56.01.7830)

3. Province – Alps – Cote D'Azur
   Commissions Regional du Film
   (Fax: 33.0.4.42.949201)

4. South of France – Var
   South of France Film Commission
   michelfcv@aol.com

Germany

1. Berlin – Brandenburg Film Commission
   www.bbfc.mind.de/SP-htm

2. Munich – FFF Film FernsehFonds Bayern GmbH
   www.fff-bayern.de

3. North Rhine – Westphalia
   Filmstiftung Nordrheim-Westfalen GmbH
   www.filmstiftung.de

4. Stuttgart
   Film Commission Stuttgart Region
   www.medien.region-stuttgart.de

Hungary
Motion Picture Public Foundation of Hungary
www.mma.hu

Houston Film Commission, The
www.neosoft.com/~yfsfilms/100-home.html

Idaho Film Bureau
www.filmidaho.org

Inland Empire Film Commission
www.filminlandempire.com/main.html

Iowa Film Office
www.state.ia.us/government/ided/film/html/fronthtml/
index/html

Isle of Man Film Commission
Email: filmcom@dti.gov.im

Liverpool Film Office
Email: lfo@dial.pipex.com

Louisiana Film Commission
www.lafilm.org

Maine Film Office
www.state.me.us/decd/film

The Maryland Film Office
www.mdfilm.state.md.us

Maui Film Office
www.filmmaui.com

Mid Wales Film Commission
www.midwalesfilm.com

Minnesota Film Board
www.mnfilm.org

Missouri Film Commission
www.ecodev.state.mo.us/film/

Nebraska Film Office
www.filmnebraska.org

New England Film
www.newenglandfilm.com/JOBS.htm

New Mexico Film Office
www.edd.state.nm.us/FILM/index.html

New Zealand Film Commission
www.nzfilm.co.nz

North Carolina Film Office
www.ncfilm.com

Northern Ireland Film Commission
www.nifc.co.uk

Northern Screen Commission
Email: nsc@filmhelp.demon.co.uk

North Wales Film Commission
www.filmnorthwales.com

Ohio Film Commission
www.ohiofilm.org

Oregon Film & Video Office
www.oregonfilm.org

Pacific Film $ Television Commission
www.pftc.com

Providence Film Commission
www.ProvidenceRI.com/film/frame.html

Rhode Island Film Office
www.riedc.com/rifilm/rifilm.html

San Francisco Film and Video Commission
www.ci.sf.ca.us/film

San Jose Film and Video Commission
www.sanjose.org/filmvideo

Santa Cruz County Film Commission
www.santacruzfilm.org

Scottish Screen
www.scottishscreen.com/index.taf

Scottish Highlands and Islands Film
www.scotfilm.org

Singapore Film Commission
www.sfc.org.sg

South Carolina Film Office
www.scfilmoffice.com

South West Film Commission
www.swfilm.co.uk

Southeastern Connecticut Film Office
www.mysticmore.com/SECTFILM

Southwest Utah Film Commission
www.southwestutahfilm.com

Switzerland – Film Location Switzerland
www.swissfilmcommission.com

Texas Film Commission
www.governor.state.tx.us/film/hotline

Virginia Film Office
www.film.virginia.org/index2.html

Volusia County Film Office (Florida)
www.volusiafilm.org

Yorkshire Screen Commission
www.ysc.co.uk

Standard Release Forms

As a screenwriter without an agent you may be asked to sign a release form when an independent producer agrees to read your script. If so . . .

Read These Forms Carefully!

Most companies will send you one of their own forms to read and sign. Basically, these clear the producers of any threat of legal action should something similar to your script be produced by their company.

Almost every screenwriting or industry book on the market contains at least one type of release form. These vary from company to company so (again) read them carefully.

The following is a release form that I received a while back. I am including it to give you an idea of what such a form may look like. However, keep in mind they are all different. I'm not recommending that you use this form; rather, use it as a guide to compare it with other forms that you may receive.

If you are unsure about or confused by what you are signing, contact an entertainment attorney. Never sign anything you don't fully understand.

RELEASE FORM (Sample)

As of_____, _____, proposed title (if any) of material submitted:_____
_____

I am on this date submitting for possible use by,_____, my material identified herein (herein after called the "Material") in accordance with the understanding, and subject of the conditions, set forth herein. I acknowledge that the Material was created and written by me without any suggestions from you that I write or create the Material. I have attached hereto a copy of said material, a synopsis thereof, or complete description of such Material in the film or tape form. I am executing and submitting this letter in consideration for your agreement to review the Material with the express understanding that I limit my claim or rights to the features of the Material as specifically synopsized or as attached hereto:

1. Except as otherwise stated herein, I represent:

a.   That the Material is original with me;

b.   That I have the exclusive right to grant all rights in the Material; and

c.   I have exclusive rights in the title, if any, in regards to its use in connection with Material.

2. You agree that you will not use the Material unless you shall first negotiate with me compensation for such use, but I understand and agree that your use of Material containing features and elements similar to or identical

with those contained in the Material shall not obligate you to negotiate with me nor entitle me to any compensation if you determine that you have an independent legal right to use such other Material which is not derived from me (either were not originated by me, or because other persons [including your employees] have submitted or may hereafter submit material containing similar or identical features or elements which you have the right to use).

3. I hereby acknowledge that you are under no obligation to use the Material in any manner.

4. I agree that I must give you written notice by certified or registered mail at your address as set forth in the address portion of this letter, of any claim arising in connection with this agreement, within the period of time prescribed by the applicable statutes of limitation, but in no event more than ninety (90) calendar days after I acquire knowledge of the facts sufficient to put me on notice of any such claim, as an expressed condition precedent to the initiation of legal action there under. My failure to so give you written notice will be deemed an irrevocable waiver of any rights I might otherwise have with respect to such claim. I shall further withhold filing any legal action for period of thirty (30) days to investigate any claim.

5. I have retained a copy of said Material, and release from you any liability for loss or other damage to the copy or copies submitted by me.

6. I hereby state that I have read and understand this agreement; that no oral representations of any kind have been made to

me; that there are no prior or contemporaneous oral agreements in effect between us pertaining to said Material; and that this agreement states our entire understanding. Any provision or part of any provision which is void or unenforceable shall be deemed omitted and shall remain in full force or effect. This agreement shall be at all times construed so as to carry out the purpose stated herein.

_____
(signature)

_____
name (print)

_____
address

_____
city/state/zip

_____
telephone (with area code)

_____
(signature of parent/s or legal guardian/s of writer under age 18)

ACCEPTED:

By:_____

cc:_____

Collaboration Agreements

Agreements are a major part of the screenwriting process. In this section I am including a sample Collaboration Agreement for your review. The one below is a slightly revised copy of a WGA Agreement.

Collaboration Agreements are used whenever you enter into a partnership in the writing of your spec script with another writer. You would not want to write ONE word until the partnership is spelled out clearly so that there are no misunderstandings.

You may request any contract forms from the WGA by contacting their office. They will fax or mail them to you. Remember, if you enter into any of the various writer's agreements be sure to use the original forms from the WGA.

Collaboration Agreement (Sample/slightly revised)

AGREEMENT made at _____, California, by and between _____ and _____, hereinafter sometimes referred to as the "Parties".

The parties are about to write in collaboration an (original story) (treatment) (screenplay)_____(other),_____based upon_____, hereafter referred to as the "Work", and are desirous of establishing all their rights and obligations in and to said Work.

NOW, THEREFORE, in consideration of the execution of this agreement, and the undertakings of the parties as hereinafter set forth, it is agreed as follows:

1. The parties shall collaborate in the writing of the Work and upon completion thereof shall be the joint owners of the Work (or shall own the Work in the following percentages:___%).

2. Upon completion of the Work it shall be registered with the Writers Guild of America, West, Inc., as the joint Work of the parties. If the Work shall be in form such as to qualify it for copyright, it shall be registered for such copyright in the name of both Parties, and each Party hereby designates the other as his attorney-in-fact to register such Work with the United States Copyright Office.

3. It is contemplated that the Work will be completed by _____ but not later than _____, provided, however, that failure to complete the Work by such date shall not be construed as a breach of this Agreement on the part of either party.

4. It is understood that _____ (both writers are/are not "professional writers"), as that term is defined in the WGA Agreement.

It is further understood by the Parties that _____(and _____), in addition to writing services, shall perform the following additional functions in addition to writing services, shall perform the following functions in regard to the Work:

If prior to the completion of the Work, either Party shall voluntarily withdraw from the collaboration, then the other Party shall have the right to complete work alone or in conjunction with another collaborator or collaborators, and in such event the percentage of ownership, as hereinbefore provided in Paragraph 1, shall be revised by mutual agreement in writing.

5. If, prior to the completion of the Work, there shall be a dispute of any kind with respect to the Work, then the parties may terminated this Collaboration Agreement by an instrument in writing, which shall be filed with the Writers Guild of America, West, Inc. [New mediation arbitration procedure in Constitution.]

6. Any contact for the sale or other disposition of the Work, where the Work has been completed by the Parties in accordance herewith, shall require that the Work shall be attributed to the authors in the following manner:

7. Neither party shall sell, or otherwise voluntarily dispose of the Work, or his/her share therein, without the written consent of the other, which consent, however shall not be unreasonably withheld. (It is agreed that to contract on behalf of the Parties without written consent of the other, on the condition that she/he negotiated no less than for the Work.)

8. It is acknowledged and agreed that _____and_____ shall be the exclusive agents of the Parties for the purpose of sale or other disposition of the Work or any rights therein. Each such agent shall represent the Parties at the following studios only:

Agent 1_____Agent 2_____

The aforementioned agent/s shall have a period in which to sell or otherwise dispose of the Work, and if there shall be more than one agent, the aggregate commission for the sale or other disposition of the Work shall be limited to ten per cent (10%) and shall be equally divided among the agents hereinbefore designated.

If there shall be two or more agents, they shall be instructed to notify each other when they have begun negotiations for the sale or other disposition of the Work and of the terms thereof and no agent shall conclude an agreement for the sale or other disposition of the Work unless he shall have first notified the other agents thereof. If there shall be a dispute among the agents as to the sale or other disposition of the Work by any of them, the matter shall immediately be referred to the Parties, who shall determine the matter for them.

9. Any and all expenses of any kind whatsoever which shall be incurred by either or both of the Parties, in connection with the writing, registration, or sale or other disposition of the Work shall be (shared jointly/ prorated in accordance with the percentages hereinbefore mentioned in Paragraph 1.)

10. All money or other things of value derived from the sale or other disposition of the Work shall be applied as follows:

a. In payment of commissions, if any.

b. In payment of any expenses or re-imbursement of either Party for expenses paid in connection with the Work.

c. To the Parties in the proportion of their ownership.

11. It is understood and agreed that for the purposes of this Agreement the Parties shall share hereunder, unless otherwise herein stated, the proceeds from the sale of any and all other disposition of the Work and the rights and licenses therein and with respect thereto, including but not limited to the following:

a. Motion picture rights
b. Sequel rights
c. Remake rights
d. Television film rights
e. Television life rights
f. Stage rights
g. Radio rights
h. Publication rights
i. Interactive rights
j. Merchandising rights

12. Should the Work be sold or otherwise disposed of and, as an incident thereto, the Parties be employed to revise the Work or write a screenplay based thereon, the total compensation provided for in such employment agreement shall be shared by them jointly in the following proportion:

If either Party shall be unavailable for the purposes of collaborating on such revision or screenplay, then the Party who is available shall be permitted to do such revision or screenplay and shall be entitled to the full amount of compensation in connection therewith, provided, however, that in such a case the purchase price shall remain fair and reasonable, and in no event shall the Party not available for the revision or screenplay receive less than _____% of the total selling price.

13. If either Party hereto shall desire to use the Work, or any right therein or with respect thereto, in a venture in which such Party shall have a financial interest, whether direct or indirect, the Party desiring to do so shall notify the other Party of that fact and shall afford such other Party the opportunity to participate in the venture in the proportion

of such other Party's interest in the Work. If such other Party is unwilling to participate in such venture, the Party desiring to proceed therein shall be required to pay such other Party an amount equal to that which such other Party would have received if the Work or right, as the case may be, intended to be so used had been sold to a disinterested person at the price at which the same shall last have been offered, or if it shall not have been offered, at its fair market value which, in the absence of mutual agreement of the Parties, shall be determined by mediation and/or arbitration in accordance with the regulations of the Writers Guild of America, West, Inc., if permissible pursuant to the WGA, West Constitution.

14. This Agreement shall be executed in sufficient number of copies so that one fully executed copy may be, and shall be, delivered to each Party and to the Writers Guild of America, West, Inc. If any disputes shall arise concerning the interpretation or application of this Agreement, or the rights or liabilities of the Parties arising hereunder, such dispute shall be submitted to the Writers Guild of America, West, Inc. And the determination of the Guild's arbitration committee as to all such matters shall be conclusive and binding upon the Parties.

DATED this _____ day of_____, _____

Remember that the previous release form is only a sample for your reference. If you are considering such a contract, it would be wise to request the most recent copy of the WGA Collaboration Agreement.

Review Paragraph 11 in the sample form and look at all the possible avenues for you to make money on a deal. Whether or not it's your own effort or a collaboration, consider the points listed in Paragraph 11 that must be addressed in *any* deal that you consider—either a sale or an option agreement. You may want to ask for a percentage of these points when you are negotiating. For instance, when selling my script *Nowhere To Hide* (a thriller), I knew that it would most likely go to video. So I wanted a percentage of the video sales and negotiated that into my deal. By being aware of what is available in a script purchase you may be able to stand a little firmer in your negotiations. Do your homework and explore your options.

Screenplay Competitions

Since I wrote this book to offer new screenwriters various ways to break into the film industry, I want to include information on screenplay competitions. These competitions are fierce! But they still provide an opportunity to submit your work. "Placing" anywhere in the competition provides a real boost to newcomers. You don't have to place in the top three or win first place, although the money is best at the top. Money is not the most important goal here, right?

The following are some well-known competitions, their deadlines, entry fees, contacts, etc. I'm not endorsing any of them, only providing this list for your information. Before entering these or any other competitions, get in touch with the contact person/s and ask about their deadlines for your submissions.

1. **America's Best Writing Competition**
   Deadline: March 6
   Objective: To support writers of all disciplines.
   Entry fee: Screenplays: $35.; TV scripts: $25.;
   Sitcoms: $25.
   Contact: Bob Cope, Director at 407-894-9001

2. **American Cinema Foundation Screenwriting**
   Competition
   Deadline: January 31
   Objective: To reward TV and film writing that addresses fundamental social values.
   Entry fee: $30.
   Contact: www.cinemafoundation.com

3. **American Dreamer Independent Filmworks**
   Deadline: July 4th; Late deadline: August 5th
   Objective: To encourage new, groundbreaking scriptwriters [and filmmakers] to pursue careers in screenwriting.

Entry fee: Early deadline $50. Late deadline $60.
Contact: ADfilmworks.com

4. **American Screenwriters Association**
Deadline: December 31
Objective: To assist and recognize screenwriters through networking. Competition is judged by professional representatives of the film and screenwriting community.
Entry fee: $25. ASA members / $50. non-members
Contact: www.asascreenwriters.com

5. **B.M.F. Productions Annual Screenwriter's Contest**
Deadline: January 5
Objective: A new, independent film company interested in producing/promoting work of fledgling filmmakers.
Entry fee: $35.
Contact/email: MicahR3@concenfric.net

6. **Bad Kitty Films Screenplay Competition**
Deadline: unknown
Objective: Searching for scripts suitable for film production.
Entry fee: $40.
Contact: www.badkittyfilms.com

7. **BDR2000 Productions Screenplay Competition**
Deadline: January 1
Objective: To give new and inspired screenwriters a chance to have their work seen and reviewed.
Entry fee: $40.
Contact: www.bdr2000.com

8. **BlueCat Screenplay Competition**
Deadline: December 1
Objective: Annual search for the best, unsold, English language screenplay in the world.
Entry fee: $20. per two screenplays.
Contact: www.bluecatscreenplay.com

9. **Carl Washington Productions**
Deadline: February 1
Objective: "Exposure. To give writers a chance to live their dreams and make them come true. It's Hollywood and it's real tough, unless you have connections. That's where this contest comes in."
Entry fee: $40. for feature-length screenplays and $20. for short screenplays.
Contact/email: whiterain.hotmail.com

10. **Chesterfield Film Company – Writer's Film Project**
Deadline: unknown
Objective: To find talented writers.
Entry fee: $39.50
Contact: www.chesterfield-co.com

11. **CineStory Screenwriting Awards**
Deadlines: August 1 (early deadline) and October 1 (late deadline)
Objective: A national screenwriting conservatory that helps writers to develop their craft.
Entry fee: $35. (August 1) and $45. (Oct. 1).
Contact: www.cinestory.com

12. **Columbus Screenplay Discovery Awards**
Deadline: Submissions accepted monthly.
Objective: To bridge the gap between writers and the entertainment industry.
Entry fee: $55.
Contact: www.Hollywoodnetwork.com

13. **Cyclone Productions Low Budget Feature Project**
Deadline: April 1
Objective: To establish an avenue for screenwriters to obtain a feature film writing credit.
Entry fee: $50.
    Contact: www.cyclone-entertainment.com

14. **Cyclone Productions Screenwriter's Project**
Deadline: September 1
Objective: To give screenwriters of diverse back-
grounds a chance.
Entry fee: $35. for August 1 deadline and $40. for
September 1st deadline
Contact: www.cyclone-entertainment.com

15. **Cynosure Screenwriting Awards**
Deadlines: Feb. 15, March 15, and April 19
Objective: To recognize and reward quality
writing with character-driven screenplays
featuring female and minority protagonists.
Entry fees: $35. (February 15), $40. (March 15),
and $45. (April 19)
Contact: www.broadmindent.com

16. **East Coast vs. West Coast Screenplay
Competition**
Deadline: August 1
Objective: "What good is a great script if no one
knows you've written one!?"
Entry fees: Features (85-135 pages) $40. and
Shorts (under 25 pages)
Contact: Tilting@Windmill Productions

17. **Euroscript Competition**
Deadline: April 30 and October 31
Objective: Project of European Union's MEDIA II
program that helps EU screenwriters develop scripts
and run writing groups. Continuous training project.
Entry fee: 25
Contact: www.euroscript.co.uk

18. **F.O.C.U.S. Institute of Film**
Deadline: March 31
Objective: Looking for socially responsible, original,
compelling, human stories that promote positive
values and social responsibility. Material
that will arouse the human spirit.

Entry fee: $100. to submit and become a member.
Contact: www.focusinstitutoffilm.com

19. **Fade In: Screenwriting Awards**
Deadline: October 30
Objective: Industry exposure from the publishers of
Fade In Magazine.
Entry fee: $35.
Contact: www.fadeinmag.com

20. **First Draft Scriptwriting Contest**
Deadline: February 28
Objective: To help writers tune up for the bigger
script contests. Offers at least two reads and critique
sheets from both. Advancing scripts get up to 5 reads.
Entry fee: $35.
Contact: www.panam.edu/scrnwrit/

21. **Grand Valley State Short Screenplay
Competition**
Deadline: December 1
Objective: Winning script will be produced in the
GVSU Summer Film Workshop.
Entry fee: None! Scripts will not be returned.
Contact: philbinj@gvsu.edu

22. **Heart of Film Screenplay Competition**
Deadline: May 15
Objective: "To provide opportunity and recognition to
a talented new screenwriter."
Entry fee: $35.
Contact: www.austinfilmfestival.org

23. **Hollywood Final-Cut Screenplay Competition**
Deadline: August 2, 2001
Objective: A contest to acknowledge and support
quality scripts from around the world.
Entry fee: $45.
Contact: www.finalcutcontest.com

24. **Hollywood Scriptwriting Contest**
Deadline: Monthly. Postmarked by the 15th of each month.
Objective: "To provide a valuable outlet for recognizing and promoting quality scripts of undiscovered writers worldwide. Independent filmmakers now provide new writers with opportunities never before available. Aspiring writers can now get recognized and gain entry into the entertainment industry more readily."
Entry fee: $35. money order or credit card.
Contact: www.moviewriting.com

25. **Hudson Valley Film Festival**
Deadline: March 1
Objective: Brings the artistry and vision of screenwriters and filmmakers together. Celebrates the screenwriter and offers a program of feature films, documentaries, videos, and script reads.
Entry fee: $15. screenplays; $20. short films, and $25. for feature films.
Contact: www.mediaflow.com/hudsval.filmfest

26. **Illinois/Chicago Screenwriting Competition**
Deadline: April 1
Objective: To promote "local" writing talent and Illinois/Chicago as a film location.
Entry fee: $25.
Contact: 312-814-8711

27. **King Arthur Screenwriters Award**
Deadline: June 30
Objective: Dedicated to working with new writers.
Entry fee: $55.
Contact: www.kingmanfilms.com

28. **KSN Television Network Scriptwriting Contest**
Deadline: January 30

Objective: To find well-written scripts for production. Contest will yield critique/analysis of top ten scripts. Script comments/suggestions. Two-page analysis for rewrite for top 100 scripts.
Entry fee: $75. US. For contest rules/entry, $5. is applied to entry fee.
Contact: 323-962-7044

29. **Massachusetts Film Office Screenwriter's Competition**
Deadline: July 1
Objective: To promote Massachusetts filming.
Entry fee: None
Contact: 617-973-8800

30. **Maui Writers Conference Screenwriting Competition**
Deadline: June 1
Objective: To bring writers together with agents, producers, and executives—to usher new talent into the marketplace.
Entry fee: $35. by April 1st and $45. by June 1st
Contact: www.maui.net/~writers

31. **Milwaukee Int'l Independent Film Festival**
Deadline: August 15
Note: They also have a screenwriting competition.
Entry fee: $20.
Contact: mcwu@concentric.net

32. **Monterey County Film Commission Screenwriting Competition**
Deadline: January 30
Objective: To encourage new film writers and increase awareness of Monterey County to screenwriters and producers.
Entry fee: $40. if postmarked by 12/30; $50 afterwards
Contact: www.tmx.com/mcfilm
also www.tmx.com/mcfilm

33. **Morrow Screenwriting Fellowship**
Deadline: April 23
Objective: To educate and promote screenwriting in
Minnesota. Judging criteria in their application packet.
Entry fee: None
Contact/email: LChute@aol.com

34. **Nantucket Film Festival Screenplay Competition**
Deadline: March 12
Objective: To find original, feature-length screenplays
that have never been produced.
Entry fee: $40.
Contact: www.nantucketfilmfestival.org

35. **Nevada Screenwriters**
Deadline: Unknown
Objective: To promote screenwriting.
Entry fee: None
Contact: 702-393-2141

36. **Nevada Screenwriters Competition**
Deadline: April 30
Objective: Promote Nevada filming and local screen-
writing talent.
Entry fee: Nevada residents $15.; nonresidents $30.
Contact: 702-486-2711

37. **New Century Writer Awards**
Deadline: Unknown
Objective: To provide a new, valuable outlet to recognize
and develop the quality screenplays, stageplays, and
fiction of undiscovered writers. To pair up new writers
with key industry people. Seeking character-driven
stories the Hollywood studios seem to ignore.
Entry fee: $25.
Contact: www.newcenturywriter.org

38. **New Harmony Project**
Deadline: November 15

Objective: To serve writers whose work emphasizes the dignity of the human spirit.
Entry fee: None
Contact: 317-464-9405

39. **New York Screenwriter Query Letter Contest**
Deadline: July 31
Objective: Seeking out the best query letter.
Entry fee: $10.
Contact: www.nyscreenwriter.com

40. **Nicholl Fellowships In Screenwriting**
Deadline: May 1
Objective: To foster the development of the art of screenwriting.
Entry fee: $30.
Contact: www.oscars.org/nicholl/index.html

41. **Organization of Black Screenwriters' Writers Competition**
Deadline: October 15.
Objective: To help up to four talented screenwriters in their career advancement.
Entry fee: Members $25.; Non-Members $35.
Contact: www.obswriter.com

42. **Oscar Moore Prize**
Deadline: September 1
Objective: European screenwriting prize—launched in memory of film journalist, Oscar Moore.
Entry fee: Contact for details
Contact: www.lsw.org.uk/hotnews.htm

43. **Pacific Northwest Writers Conference Literary Contest**
Deadline: February 13
Objective: To help writers attain professional standards.
Entries: Judged on literary quality and market-ability.
Entry fee: Members $25.; Non-Members $35.
Contact: www.pnwa.org/

44. **Page One: Fade In Scriptwriting Competition**
Deadline: October 31
Objective: They look for a "fun time" on page one of a
script: a killer opening, an incredible image, an
outrageous character, the visual metaphor that defines
the movie, or even one that speaks on its own.
Entry fee: $20. per submission
Contact: www.screenwritersgroup.com

45. **Praxis Film Development Workshop**
Deadline: June 30 and October 30
Objective: They want dramatic scripts, preferably to be
produced in Canada.
Entry fee: $65.
Contact: www.praxisfilm.com

46. **Providence Film Foundation Screenwriting
Competition**
Deadline: May 15
Objective: Sponsored by Providence Film Foundation,
Providence Film Commission, and Mayor Cianci.
Entry fee: $25. per submission
Contact: www.providenceri.com/film

47. **Samuel Goldwyn Writing Awards Competition for
Theater, Film & Television**
Deadline: May
Objective: To support student screenwriters at any
campus of the University of California.
Entry fee: None
Contact: 310-825-9734

48. **Santa Fe Writers Project**
info@sfwintersproject.com

49. **Screenwriter's Showcase Awards**
Deadline: April 1, August 1, December 1
Objective: Provides writers with tools they need to
succeed!
Sponsors include: Dramatica Pro, ScriptThing, and
National Creative Registry.

Entry fee: $20.

Contact: www.screenwritersutopia.com/contest.html

50. **Script Connection's Annual Screenplay Competition**
Deadline: July
Objective: To give talented new writers another way to "get connected" within the industry by exposing the winners to major Hollywood producers and agents for possible option/representation. *Every* entrant receives a detailed analysis of his or her script.
Entry fee: $75. ($50. for starving artist/students)
Contact: home.pacbell.net/marion1

51. **Slamdance Screenplay Competition**
Deadline: Early one is March 19; Main one is May 21; Late one is July 23.
Objective: To support new filmmakers on an ongoing basis.
Entry fee: $45. March, $50. May, $60. July
Contact: www.slamdance.com

52. **Taos Land & Film Screenplay Contest**
Deadline: January 25
Objective: To find quality screenplays to produce. And to put finalists in touch with agents and producers.
Entry fee: $75 ($50 for students and starving artists)
Contact: www.taoslandfilm.com

53. **Telluride IndieFest**
Deadline: August 1
Objective: A unique festival/seminar dedicated to the advancement of independent film/videomaking and screenwriting.
Entry fee: Screenplays $40.
Contact: telluridemm.com/indifest.html

54. **Twisted Kittens Screenplay Competition**
Deadline: January 31 (early); February 28 (late)
Objective: "To reward excellent, innovative writing and ideas with cash (for the bills) and kudos (for the soul)."

Possible leads for production for competition finalists.
Entry fee: $25 early entry; $35 late entry
Contact: mzthang@concentric.net

55. **Unique Television Competition**
Deadline: Twice yearly, June 1 and December 1
Objective: To discover fresh writing talent for TV/cable.
Entry fee: $45.
Contact: www.geocities.com/TelevisionCity/stage/5563

56. **Virginia Governor's Screenwriting Competition**
Deadline: July 10
Objective: To help Virginia screenwriters and to promote filmmaking in Virginia.
Entry fee: None
Contact: www.film.virginia.org

57. **Walt Disney Studios Fellowship Program**
Deadline: Between April 1 and April 19
Objective: To seek out and employ culturally and ethnically-diverse new writers.
Entry fee: None
Contact: www.abcnewtalent.disney.com/

58. **Warner Bros. Comedy Writers Workshop**
Deadline: unknown
Objective: To develop talented sitcom writers.
Entry fee: $25 application fee; workshop cost $495
Contact: sitcomwksp@aol.com

59. **Writer's Network Screenplay Competition**
Deadline: May 15
Objective: To give new and talented writers the chance to pursue a career in film and television. Judging is done by WGA Signatory Agencies.
Entry fee: $35
Contact: writersnet@aol.com

Trade Publications

Part of your writing business involves keeping up-to-date with what's going on in the film industry—its trends, what the "players" are doing, who the "comers" are, etc. One way to keep current is by reading as much as possible about the industry. You may not live in Los Angeles, but you can still read the trade publications. (These are available at all major book stores.)

The following list includes some of the publications that I believe are among the best. Some of the most popular ones are available in some capacity on the Internet.

Daily Variety
700 Wilshire Boulevard, #120, Los Angeles, CA 90036
Phone: 213-857-6600

The Hollywood Reporter
6715 Sunset Boulevard, Hollywood, CA 90028
Phone: 213-464-7411

The Hollywood Scriptwriter
1626 North Wilcox Avenue, #385, Hollywood, CA 90028

StoryNotes
15721 Brighton Avenue, #D, Gardena, CA, 90247

Written By (WGA)
8955 Beverly Boulevard, Los Angeles, CA 90068

Fade In Magazine
c/o: Writer's Network, 289 South Robinson Blvd, Suite 465, Beverly Hills, CA 90211-2834

Freelance Screenwriter's Forum
P.O. Box 7, Baldwin, MD 21013
A national newsletter which emphasizes services to writers outside of Los Angeles.

Filmmaker, The Magazine of Independent Film
1625 Olympic Boulevard, Santa Monica, CA 90404-3822

Premiere Magazine
P.O. Box 55387, Boulder, CO 80323-5387

The Ross Report, Television Index, Inc.
40-29 27th Street, Long Island City, NY 11101
Phone: 718-937-3990

Electronic Media
740 Rush Street, Chicago, IL 60611
A weekly publication for information on alternative markets:
syndication, cable, and regional television.

Emmy Magazine
c/o: Academy of Television Arts & Sciences
3500 West Olive, Suite 700, Burbank, CA 91505
Phone: 818-953-7575

Drama-Logue
P.O. Box 38771, Los Angeles, CA 90038
Phone: 213-464-5079

Creative Screenwriting
816 E. Street North East, Suite 201, Washington DC, 20002
Phone: 202-543-3438

Women In Film Newsletter
6464 Sunset Boulevard, Suite 530, Los Angeles, CA 90028

Screenwrite NOW!
P.O. Box 7, Long Green Pike, Baldwin, MD 21013-2456

New York Screenwriter
545 8th Avenue, Suite 410, New York, NY 10018

Film Industry Organizations

Support during the writing and marketing process is necessary to your career and your growth as a professional. This is even more important when you don't live in Hollywood. If there are no screenwriting groups in your area, why not start a group of your own? Run ads. Create and distribute flyers in your local library. You may be pleasantly surprised by the number of writers who respond. Contact the film commission in your state to find organizations in your area.

Academy of Motion Picture Sciences
8949 Wilshire Boulevard, Beverly Hills, CA 90212
Phone: 213-656-8990

Atlanta Screenwriters Group
www.gtf.org/hrivnak/script/asg.shtml

Directors Guild of America
7950 Sunset Boulevard, Los Angeles, CA 90046
Phone: 310-289-2000; Fax: 310-289-2029

   – In Chicago
   400 North Michigan Avenue, Suite 307
   Phone: 312-644-5050; Fax: 312-644-5776
   – In New York
   110 West 57th Street, New York, NY 10019
   Phone: 212-581-0370; Fax: 212-581-1441
   – In Florida
   4000 Hollywood Blvdd, Suite 265-S, Hollywood, FL 33021
   Phone: 305-981-0233; Fax: 305-963-6155

Independent Feature Project/West
1625 Olympic Boulevard, Santa Monica, CA 90404
Phone: 310-292-8832

Independent Feature Project
104 West 29th Street, 12th FL, New York, NY 10012

New Voices Screenwriters Group
www.clubhomepage.com/cgi-bin/
   login.cgi?type=club&acct=new voices

Northern California Writers & Artists
P.O. Box 163074, Sacramento, CA 95816

Producers Guild of America, Inc.
400 South Beverly Drive, Suite 211, Beverly Hills, CA 90212
Phone: 213-557-0807

The Screen Actors Guild
7065 Hollywood Blvd, Hollywood, CA 90028
Phone: 213-465-4600

The Scriptwriters Network
11684 Ventura Blvdd, Suite 508, Studio City, CA 91604

Virginia Screenwriters Forum
www.earthlink.net/~scriptwritr/virginiascreenwriters.html

Women In Film
6464 Sunset Blvdd, Suite 660, Los Angeles, CA 90028
Phone: 213-463-6040
Dedicated to recognizing and furthering the role of women in filmmaking. They conduct seminars, film festivals, and classes, and they publish a monthly magazine.

Writers Guild of America, West
7000 West Third Street, Los Angeles, CA 90048-4329
Phone: 213-951-4000

Writers Network
289 South Robinson Blvd, Suite 465, Beverly Hills, CA 90211
If you feel completely lost and want to get in touch, contact: Location Update, P.O. Box 17106, North Hollywood, CA 91615. A regional source of screenwriting groups in your state and the workshops offered. They also publish a magazine.

Author's Note: If you want your local screenwriting group added to this list when this book is updated, send your group's name, information, Web and email addresses, and/or mailing address to: Andrea Leigh Wolf, P.O. Box 2385, Fair Oaks, CA 95628-2385.

Web Connections For Screenwriters

Being connected to the Internet is the next best thing to being in Hollywood. The World Wide Web may offer many golden opportunities for screenwriters, no matter where they live on the planet. They may gain access to Hollywood insiders as well as contact other screenwriters around the globe.

The following list provides some websites that may be useful. New ones are being developed all the time, so keep exploring!

Absolute Write
www.absolutewrite.com
An excellent site for writers in general.

Academy of Motion Picture Arts & Sciences
www.oscars.org

Academy of Television Arts & Sciences
www.emmys.org

Albany Intl. Short Film Festival
Email: aisff@pass-cine.com

American Film Institute
www.afionline.org

American Screenwriter's Association
www.asascreenwriters.com

American Zoetrope
www.zoetrope.com
Francis Ford Coppola's Production Company has one of the best websites on the Internet today. AZ offers an excellent site for new screenwriters who may benefit from reading and reviewing spec scripts by other screenwriters. After reading and reviewing four scripts posted by other screenwriters, you may post your own script in the hope of getting valuable feedback of your work. Participants

are then allowed to re-post their revised scripts for further reviews. As an added bonus, the AZ staff reads the scripts with the highest, favorable reviews. This is one way a newcomer may get a script into a major production company.

Atlanta Screenwriters Group
www.gtf.org/hrivnak/script/asg.shtml

Baseline
www.pkbaseline.com

Big Screen Biz
www.bigscreenbiz.com/Directory

Cinestory
www.Cinestory.com

Copyright Site
http://www.lcweb.loc.gov/

"Craft of Writing – 'Goofs & Gaffes' "
www.wga.org/craft/writers.html
Read this excellent article by the WGA.

Directors Guild of America
www.dga.org/

Done Deal
www.scriptsales.com/
This site has recently sold scripts by title—with a log line, the writer, the agent who sold the script, the studio, amount of sale, genre, and other pertinent information about the project, such as who has been cast. The site also lists agencies and production companies.

Drew's Script-O-Rama
www.script-o-rama.com
www.script-o-rama.com/tv/tvscript.shtml
This site has many television scripts.
Scripts available to print out or just read on-line.

Fade In Magazine Online
www.fadeinmag.com

Feature Film Project
www.ifpwest.org

Film Festivals
http://dir.yahoo.com/Entertainment/Movies_and_Film/
Film_Festivals

Filmmaker Magazine
www.filmmaker.com

Fine Line Features
www.flf.com/homepage.html
A great site! With many scripts available for downloading.
And the screenplays are preserved in their original format.

Florida Film Festival
www.enzian.org

From Query to Sale
www.mindspring.com/~spacklebeast/querytosale/
A great site for people who have finished their first
script and don't know what to do with it.

From Script to Screen
www.fromscript2screen.com
An informative site.

Great Research Links
www.wga.org/leftnav.html

Hollywood Creative Directory
www.hollyvision.com

Hollywood Live!
www.hollywoodnetwork.com

Hollywood Network
www.hollwoodnetwork.com/dealmaking
www.hollywoodnetwork.com/live

www.hollywoodnetwork.com/moviestore

Hollywood Online
www.hollywood.com

Hollywood Reporter
www.hollywoodreporter.com

Hollywood Scripts
I could not find a website listing for this company. However, to buy screenplays you may order their catalog. Send $1 check or money order to: Hollywood Scripts, 5514 Satsuma Ave., Suite A, North Hollywood, CA 91601.

Hollywood Scriptwriter
www.hollywoodscriptwriter.com
They have an email Bulletin.

Hong Kong Intl. Film Market
www.tdc.org.hk

Horror Writers Association
www.horror.org

"How They Got Their First Break"
www.wga.org/craft/AlanBrennert.html
www.wga.org/craft/ErikBork.html

ifilm ("the place for Internet films")
www.ifilm.com
This site offers a free, informative online newsletter.
Independent Film Production
www.indycine.com

Independent Feature Projects, West
www.hollyvision.com/IFPwest/ifhome.html

Independent Filmmakers
www.aivf.org/index_enhanced.html

"Interactive Writing"
www.wga.org/ia/index.html
To receive their e-newsletter list, write to their email
address: join-wga@sparklist.com.

Internet Screenwriter's Network
www.screenwriters.com/hn/writing/swroom/board.html

LA Times On-line
www.latimes.com/

Law Cybercenter
www.hollywoodnetwork.com/Law/insider/board.html

LucasArts Entertainment Company
www.lucasarts.com

The Mad Screenwriter
www.madscreenwriter.com

Mark Litwak FAMOUS Entertainment Attorney
www.marklitwak.com/index.html
This site has valuable information on how to make film
and television deals and how to protect yourself legally.

Mandy's Film and Television Production Directory
www.mandy.com

Mark's Screenwriting Page
www.geocities.com/hollywood/theater/6448/

MCA/Universal
www.mca.com/tv/index.html

MGM Home Video
www.mgm.com

MGM Lion's Den
www.mgmua.com

MGM Television
www.mgmua.com/outerlimits.index.html

Miramax Cafe
www.miramax.com

Monterey County Film Commission
www.tmx.com/mcfilm/

MovieBytes
www.moviebytes.com
Free email newsletter, listing contest deadlines reminders, contest news, screenplay marketing opportunities, etc.

MovieMaker Magazine
www.moviemaker.com

Mr. Showbiz
http://mrshowbiz.go.com

New York Screenwriter
www.nyscreenwriter.com
The screenwriter's guide to making it.
The New York Screenwriter Monthly online.
Free e-newsletter with contest information, etc.

New York Underground Film Festival
Email: Nyuff@aol.com

Online Communicator: Screenwriting
www.communicator.com/writfilm.html

Paramount Online Studio
www.paramount.com

Production
www.screenwriter.com/insider/production.html

Production Weekly
www.productionweekly.com

Professional Screenwriter's Network
www.screenwriter.com/insider/psnhome.html

Romance Writers of America
www.rwanational.com

SCREEN-L
www.tcf.ua.edu/screensite/

Screen Talk
www.screentalk.org/
A great new E-zine that covers the biz!

Screenscribe Home Page
www.rt66.com/cedge

Screenspec
www.mysterywriters.org/library/screenwriting.html

Screenwriter
www.nyscreenwriter.com

Screenwriter's Cyberia
www.members.aol.com/swcyberia/
Hundreds of fantastic links.

Screenwriter's Online Cooperative
www.members.aol.com/socwebsite/index.html
A craft and career development group for screenwriters.

Screenwriter's Utopia Page
www.screenwritersutopia.com
An excellent site for screenwriters.

Screenwriting Help
www.concentric.net/~pcbc/

Script Shack
www.scriptshack.com/shop/enter.html
They sell scripts.

Script World

www.screenwriter.com/scriptworld.html
They sell scripts.

Scripts-Onscreen

www.scripts-onscreen.com

SCRNWRIT FAQ

www.hollywoodnet.com/ScrnFAQ/ScrnFAQV.html

Script Secrets

www.scriptsecrets.com
"Tips of the Day."

Sisters In Crime

www.sistersincrime.org
This site offers research information. A research page allows direct access to some of the best search tools on the Internet. Many useful sites are linked to this one.

Sony

www.sony.com

Spec Screenplay Sales Directory

www.hollywoodlitsales.com
See what the industry is buying!

SteppinStone Entertainment

www.steppinstone.com

Studio Coverage

www.screenwriter.com/insider/sc.html
Script analysis, critiques, and reports are on this site, which follow the studio system.

"Tools of the Trade"

www.wga.org/tools/index.html
A great article from the WGA.

Turner
www.turner.com

Turner Home Entertainment
www.turner.com/theindex.html

Twentieth Century Fox
www.foxworld.com/index_frames.html

Walt Disney Studios
www.disney.com

Warner Sisters Productions
www.warnersisters.com

Western Writers of America
www.westernwriters.org

Writers Guild of America
www.wga.org
This site offers an excellent, free E-newsletter filled with valuable information and industry news. A "must see" site!

Wine Country Film Festival
www.winecountryfilmfest.com

Women in Film
http://wif.org/home/index.html

WordPlay
www.wordplayer.com

Writer's Computer Store
www.hollywoodnetwork.com/writerscomputer

"Writing Low-Budget Films"
www.communicator.com/scripttip.html
This site has an excellent article to help beginning screenwriters develop scripts that appeal to independent

producers' low budgets. It explains what raises budgets to prohibitive levels, possibly causing good scripts to be rejected. Read how to avoid making such mistakes.

Written By
www.wga.org/WrittenBy
The WGA magazine

Writers Write: Screenwriting
www.writerswrite.com/screenwriting/

Young Filmmakers Showcase
www.neosoft.com/~yfsfilms

Script Doctors

This book would be an incomplete marketing tool if I failed to mention the importance of the Script Doctor. An effective script doctor will evaluate your script with a professional eye for character development, plot points, story structure, dialogue, and scene transition.

Should you consider using a script doctor? That depends on how serious you are about a screenwriting career.

It's difficult to be objective about your own work. Even if friends read your script and say it's great, how much do they know about what makes a selling script? But if you submit a script prematurely, it could be fatal to your career because industry insiders rarely consider a script twice. This is when you turn to an industry professional—a script doctor.

You've already invested a large amount of time in writing your Calling Card Script. If you're really serious, then paying a good script doctor will be worth it, and the rewards could be endless.

Script doctors aren't cheap, but a good script doctor can mean the difference between rejection and an insider's interest. And after all, that's the name of the game, isn't it?

Script doctors don't submit your script to a studio, an agent, or a producer. They won't rewrite your script for you either. What they will do is tell you the truth, pointing out both the weak and strong points of your script and making suggestions for character development, plot structure, dialog, and smooth scene transitions. They will suggest changes that will make your script work where it didn't work before.

If you do send your script to a script doctor, it will almost certainly require even more revisions. (Remember: screenwriting is rewriting.) That said, script doctors have now become Hollywood's newest specialty, and they are opening offices everywhere. Some of them are qualified and some are not. With so much at stake, you'll have to do your homework. Don't be afraid to ask them questions. Always send a query letter, and ALWAYS ask for client recommendations. Find out about their background in screenwriting and if they have ever written a script before. Even when you learn the answers, to whom do you turn?

I've taken the liberty of listing a few script doctors who I know personally to help you get started. Highly qualified script doctors are pricey, but how much are you willing to pay to make your script the best it can be? You want your script to stand out because of its quality, not for the lack of it. Hiring a script doctor is an investment in your future career.

Write your script, polish it, and when you feel it's the best that it can be, send it to a script doctor to find out how much help it needs. You may be amazed. Good script doctors are worth their weight in gold.

The script doctors listed below are well known in the film community. I feel comfortable recommending them to you.

Dr. Linda Seger (also known as "Hollywood's Screenwriting Guru") is the author of the highly acclaimed book, *Making a Good Script Great*. Dr. Seger has been in the script consulting business since 1983 and teaches the craft of screenwriting all over the world. To reach Dr. Seger:
> 2038 Louella Avenue, Venice, CA 90291
> Phone: 310-390-1951; Fax: 310-398-7541
> Email: lsseger@aol.com
> Website: www.screentalk.org/art012.htm

Dara Marks is a Script Consultant who received her training under Dr. Linda Seger. Dara was rated #1 Script Analyst by *Creative Screenwriting Magazine*, Mar/Apr 1999 issue. You may contact Dara:
> Phone: 805-640-1307 or Fax: 805-640-1239
> Email: dara@ojai.net
> Website: www.DaraMarks.net

Dr. Rachel Ballon is an international script doctor. Dr. Linda Seger also trained her. She is the author of two books: *Blueprint for Writing* and *The Writer's Sourcebook*. Contact Dr. Ballon at:

    Phone/Fax: 310-479-0048
    Email: Rachwrite@aol.com
    Website: www. rachelballon.com

James Dalessandro is a screenwriting teacher and script doctor. After he sold *Breakin* he sold five screenplays in a row. He also founded the Santa Cruz Poetry Festival, which has become the nation's largest literary event. James's last script sale was the epic *1906* to Warner Brothers. People actually drive hundreds of miles to take his screenwriting class in San Francisco, and there is always a waiting list. Even the most experienced screenwriter can benefit from taking a class from James Dalessandro. He cares about new writers and he's consumed with a passion for the art of screenwriting. He's one of the few professional screenwriters teaching screenwriting. He is also a script doctor who knows what it's like to labor over a screenplay. He's a professional who makes time to teach others, and he's great at it. You may contact James Dalessandro at:

    Phone: 415-457-1959
    Email: Rimbaud40@aol.com

Ray Robinson takes time from his busy production schedule to be a script doctor. He has over fifteen years experience in the film industry. He began his career as an associate producer for Valstar Productions, where he helped develop *When the Full Moon Rises*, *Cry for Justice*, and *Inner Blues*. You may reach Mr. Robinson at:

    Prodigy Entertainment
    Post Office Box 4498
    Mountain View, CA 94040
    Phone: 415-681-0796

After You Sell Your Script

Once a spec script is sold, it follows a path which can be somewhat confusing to a newcomer. The list below will help you to follow the progress of a spec script and to understand possible delays. In other words, a project usually follows this path:

1. **ACQUISITION**
   Purchase of the story. The story may be based on a literary work, a play, a magazine or newspaper article, a book, or an original screenplay. The purchaser then checks the copyright to see if it's free and clear, and if it is actually the property of the writer who is making the deal. The option agreement is signed. The acquisition agreement is signed.

2. **DEVELOPMENT**
   Acquire development financing, develop idea/concept, write a one-line description, and decide on the basic story outline. Write the synopsis, the treatment and then the screenplay. Write a first draft, polish it and rewrite the final screenplay. Register the script with the WGA and copyright it.

3. **PACKAGING**
   Casting, packaging agent, packaging attorney, packaging service, partial financing, director commitment, star commitments, producer deferments, director deferments, star deferments, lab deferments, first draft script breakdown, production board, distribution agreements (if any), pre-sales (if any), production budget, completion bond, and the producer/director undertakings.

4. **PRODUCTIONS FINANCING**
   Studio, negative pickup agreement, pre-sales agreements, corporate financing, joint venture, co-productions, limited partnership, loans, blocked funds, facilities deals, tax shelters, debt capitalization, currency deals, grants, and subsidies.

5. PRE-PRODUCTIONS

During "pre-production," the "shooting script" is written and the script is approved. The following agreements are negotiated, written, and signed: release forms, the director's agreement, deal memos, crew/performer agreements, location and stage agreements, producer's liability insurance, chain of title agreements, producer's agreements, film and sound lab agreements, equipment rental agreements.

6. PRINCIPAL PHOTOGRAPHY

At this point the following are all in place: the producer, director, director's cast list, cast/extras, film stock/sound stock, editing, location list, studio rental, publicity, insurance, fees, and taxes. Transportation is arranged. The following are also arranged: staff, set design, equipment rentals, lab film processing letter, dailies (rushes), second unit, post-production schedule.

7. POST-PRODUCTION

Editing, dialogue replacement, music, special effects, optical effects, sound effects, titles, stage recording, pick-up photography, pre-mix session, and dirty dupes.

8. DELIVERY

Laboratory access letter, film credits, delivery schedule, laboratory letter, final screenplay, shooting script, publicity material, credit statement, photographs, final answer print, original picture negative, inter-positive, television cover shots, sound album material, inter-negatives, main and end titles, music, dialogue and sound items, film and soundtrack materials, screen credits, dialogue, action continuity, MPAA (Motion Picture Academy of Arts) certificate, certificate of insurance, residual information, title and copyright reporting, composite optical soundtrack negative, work print, and out-takes (cutouts).

Glossary

Following are some film industry terms and jargon:

A Go—a project will get produced or get a "green light."

A-list—top talent in the industry.

Above the line—refers to talent (the writer, director, actors, producer); negotiable expenses.

Writers Guild of America Arbitration Board—panel who determines a writer's credits.

Associate Producer—does one or more producer functions, delegated to be "the producer."

Back End—profits after a film is released.

Below the Line—production costs (for gaffers, grips, set designers, make-up people, etc.)

Big Guns—established writers, producers, directors.

Break Down—(1) the producer does an analysis of the script for costs, shooting schedules, etc.; (2) a list of the cast (actors) circulated to agents on a daily basis.

Calling Card—a script that gets you in the door; your "calling card" script.

Commercial—a project that has the potential to draw big money, top actors, and big box office returns.

Co-Producer—one of two or more producers on a team.

Coverage—report of a script by a reader.

Cut Offs—producer or network decides not to take up the option.

Deal—the contract.

Deal Breaker—a point in negotiations that can break the deal.

Delivery of Story—the writer turns in the story outline.

Development—the first phase of the production of a project: development financing, acquisition of the idea/concept, creation of a one-line description and the basic story outline; the synopsis, treatment, screenplay, first draft, polish, rewrite, final screenplay are written; the script is registered with the WGA; the script is copyrighted.

Development Deal—a writer is hired to develop a screenplay from an idea.

Development Hell—the period between the option of project and a green light; or, after a script is sold and before pre-production; or a problem develops with the script or financing, which can halt the project or slow it down.

Development Person—hired to find writers or a script.

Executive Producer—supervises one or more producers.

Film Order—"a go" to shoot film.

First Look Deal—when a studio buys the rights to the first option on any project that the writer develops.

Flavor of the Month—newest talent with *heat*.

Giving Notes—critiquing a script.

Green Light—A "Yes!" to do a project.

Grip—works in film production as a laborer.

Gross—total amount of money received *before* expenses.

Guarantee—contract assurance that a writer will receive the amount agreed upon, whether or not the script is produced.

Heat—if a writer's last project was a success.

If/Come—similar to an option (*If* I can sell the project, you can *come* to work for us.

Line Producer—supervises physical production.

Location—place other than a studio where filming occurs.

Logline—one-line description of plot.

Low Budget—for a studio this is $6,000,000 or less; for the WGA it is $2,500,000 or less.

Minimum—least amount of money that the WGA members are allowed to work for.

MOW—Movie-of-the-Week.

Notes—feedback to a writer when changes are needed.

On Spec—writing a script for no money up-front.

Option—a fee paid by a producer to gain the rights to shop a writer's script.

Page One Rewrite—a complete rewrite of a script.

Pay or Play— a guarantee that the writer will get paid.

Pitch—an oral synopsis of script.

Plugged In—close association with those in power.

Points—percentage points of film earnings.

Polish—final draft of a script.

Post Production—the work done *after* the completion of principal photography.

Pre-Production—an assignment of shoot date and the first day of principal photography.

Producer—plans, coordinates, and supervises everything from script to screen.

Punching Up A Script—making the script livelier or funnier.

Reader—a studio employee who weeds through and reads submitted scripts. Also known as an "analyst."

Registration—a form of protection against plagiarism.

Release Form—a form that a writer (who does not have an agent) might be asked to sign before submitting a script for consideration.

Residuals—money that writers receive every time their films or television shows are shown.

Revisions—rewrites by a writer on a script.

Royalties—money writers receive when their shows are shown. (same as residuals),

Scenario—detailed synopsis.

Signatory—parties that have agreed to the Writers Guild Minimum Basic.

Sitcom—situation comedy.

Slug line—describes a change of scene using these abreviations: INT. (interior) / EXT. (exterior) – (LOCATION) – DAY/NIGHT). It describes the scene direction, whether the scene is interior or exterior, and whether it's day or night. On shooting scripts there is more information on the slug lines.

Speculation—writing a screenplay or script without a contract.

Solicited—scripts submitted by an agent; requested material.

Step Deal—a writer is paid in segments as each part of the script is completed, and as the project moves from development to principal photography.

Step Outline—condensed treatment or outline.

Story Conference—a meeting to develop a script; it may involve the writer, producer, executive producer, and director.

Story Line—the main thrust of the plot.

Trades—publications relating to the film industry.

Treatment—a short story written in present tense; story outline.

Turnaround—the script has been paid for, however, the studio decides *not* to produce it.

Unsolicited—scripts that were received but not requested; writers must query first.

Writers Guild of America—the trade union.

About The Author

Andrea Leigh Wolf, the daughter of a Broadway actress, was introduced to the arts at an early age. In her teens she traveled extensively throughout Europe, visiting every country except Spain. She spent summers in Germany and lived with an aunt and uncle in a 17th century castle in Bavaria.

Even before she could write, Andrea fell in love with movies. She has always loved to write and tell stories. Many people enjoyed her letters. She earned high grades on essays and term papers, and graduated with a major in English and a minor in history.

Andrea usually has a pen and paper in hand and writes in long-hand. She often imagines storylines (more stories than she will ever have time to write). She completed her first novel (an 850-page historical romance, *Jonathan's Destiny*) before her fifteenth birthday. Stored in her "Hope Chest" until 1978, it now resides on her office shelf and awaits revision.

She wrote about a real-life family tragedy. Six months after the birth of their first child, she and her husband were held hostage for more than three hours, while the perpetrator continually held a .45 automatic to their heads. He held the baby and threatened to shoot her if she cried. Fortunately, she didn't wake up. They all survived that terrible night. (In 2000, she and her husband happily celebrated their 36th wedding anniversary.)

In 1988 Andrea began her lifelong dream of becoming a professional screenwriter. She attended numerous screenwriting workshops and lectures. And she read every book on the subject that she could find. While learning the craft of writing for the Big Screen, she wrote newspaper articles/special features for the *Sacramento Union*. She had a stint as a movie critic with her own column, "Movie Moments With Andrea," for *Amazing Experiences Magazine* and reviewed science fiction films. As the magazine began to consume more of her writing time, she resigned and began pursuing screenwriting full-time.

Since 1988 Andrea has met some major players in the film industry; some have graciously taken an interest in her writing. Many of them continue to offer advice and support.

Andrea has now optioned four feature scripts, sold her first spec script, *Nowhere To Hide*, currently in development. She was hired to write *Just Enuff*, for a Northern California entertainment company. She has never used an agent. She has enjoyed developing her marketing and networking skills. After hearing horror stories about other writers and their agents, she experienced one herself.

After responding to an ad in the trades, she was invited to work for an Italian film company in Milan. Not knowing much about the business at that time (1989), she found and asked for an agent's advice. She asked for the amount that the agent had suggested. This request came after the company had offered to pay for her first class accommodations, round-trip air fare, and all expenses during her stay in Italy. The company had asked what salary she would expect. Not knowing how much to ask for, she called for the agent's advice. When she related all that the agent had recommended, the Italian film company dropped her offer instantly. She had asked for too much. When she told the agent that she had asked for too much, he said, "Of course, you were asking too much! They were supposed to negotiate with you!" They didn't bring up negotiations and neither did she. So, unfortunately, she lost the deal and the chance of a lifetime.

After that experience, Andrea decided to depend on herself and rely on what she could learn from the business. She would not turn her opportunities or decisions over to someone who had no stake in her career. She was burned so badly that she wouldn't be able to trust another agent after that. However, she says, "Never say never. In the film business, you never want to close doors."

Andrea has attended many writers' workshops and seminars throughout the United States. She attended classes at Pierce College in Woodland Hills; a conference called "The Art and Business of Screenwriting in New York"; classes at California State University in Northridge and the American River College in Sacramento; and classes at the College of the Pacific in Stockton. She has attended lectures by industry legends—such as Danny Simon, Richard Pierce, Lew Hunter, Mike Werb, Aaron Sorken, J. Kenneth Rotcop, Irving Cooper, Linda Seger, and Steve Allen.

Andrea is grateful for the many film industry professionals who have been supportive of her—who have offered their insight and invaluable advice. While there are some "sharks" in the Hollywood "sea"; not all sharks bite. She prefers to be honest and upfront with everyone she meets.

Currently she is working on her 35th screenplay; she has rewritten the current one nine times. She writes full-time, almost daily; she seldom writes less than twelve to sixteen hours per day. When she's on a roll she writes all night long. She enjoys writing with a deadline approaching and tends to create them for herself since she writes best under pressure.

Andrea appreciates her supportive family. Her husband works hard so that she can stay home and write. He told her, "You have done a great job raising our family. Now it's your turn. Shoot for the stars!"

Final Note

If you want to share your suggestions, successes, failures, tips, comments, etc., or if you're an independent film or TV producer who would like to be included in future editions of this book or on our websites, please write or send email to:

Andrea Leigh Wolf
P.O. Box 2385
Fair Oaks, CA 95628

Email: awolf@pacbell.net

Books Available From Robert D. Reed Publishers

Please include payment with orders. Send indicated book/s to:

Name:_____

Address:_____

City:_____ State:_____ Zip:_____

Phone:(____)_____ E-mail:_____

Titles and Authors	Unit Price
Gotta Minute? Sell Your Screenplay: Your Guide to the Independent Film and Television Producer by Andrea Leigh Wolf	$15.95
Gotta Minute? How to Look & Feel Great! by Marcia F. Kamph, D.C., M.S.	11.95
Gotta Minute? Practical Tips for Abundant Living: The ABC's of Total Health by Tom Massey, Ph.D., N.D.	9.95
Gotta Minute? Yoga for Health, Relaxation & Well-being by Nirvair Singh Khalsa	9.95
Gotta Minute? Ultimate Guide of One-Minute Workouts for Anyone, Anywhere, Anytime! by Bonnie Nygard, M.Ed. & Bonnie Hopper, M.Ed.	9.95
A Kid's Herb Book For Children Of All Ages by Lesley Tierra, Acupuncturist and Herbalist	19.95
Saving The Soul of Medicine by M. A. Mahony, M.D.	21.95
House Calls: How we can all heal the world one visit at a time by Patch Adams, M.D.	11.95
500 Tips For Coping With Chronic Illness by Pamela D. Jacobs, M.A.	11.95

Enclose a copy of this order form with payment for books. Send to the address below. Shipping & handling: $2.50 for first book plus $1.00 for each additional book. California residents add 8.5% sales tax. We offer discounts for large orders.

Please make checks payable to: Robert D. Reed Publishers. Total enclosed: $_____. See our Web site for more books!

Robert D. Reed Publishers
750 La Playa, Suite 647, San Francisco, CA 94121
Phone: 650-994-6570 • Fax: 650-994-6579
Email: 4bobreed@msn.com • www.rdrpublishers.com